The Newbie Investor

Navigating-the-Stock-Market

SAGAR VAISHYA

ISBN
Paperback 979-8-89929-428-0
Hardcase 979-8-89929-429-7

Contents

1

Understanding the Stock Market Basics

1.1 What is the Stock Market?

The stock market, often viewed as a labyrinth of financial jargon and complex concepts, is fundamentally a marketplace where ownership in companies is bought and sold. For anyone aspiring to build wealth through investing, understanding this marketplace is essential. Beyond facilitating stock exchanges, the stock market plays a crucial role in the global economy by allowing companies to raise capital and enabling investors to share in the growth of businesses.

To truly grasp the stock market, one must first understand stocks themselves. Stocks are essentially claims on a company's assets and earnings. When you buy a share of stock, you acquire a small piece of that company. This ownership not only entitles you to a portion of the company's profits—usually distributed as dividends—but also grants you voting rights in certain corporate matters. As of 2025, the World Federation of Exchanges reports that there are over 60 major stock exchanges worldwide, with the New York Stock Exchange (NYSE) and NASDAQ, being the most prominent in the United States. National Stock Exchange(NSE) In India. These exchanges act as platforms where buyers and sellers converge to trade shares, ensuring liquidity and facilitating price discovery.

Stock trading primarily occurs on these regulated exchanges. When a company opts to go public, it typically does so through an Initial Public Offering (IPO), which allows it to sell shares to the public for the first time. This process not only generates capital for the company but also offers investors a chance to invest in its future growth. Once shares are listed on an exchange, they can be traded among investors, creating a dynamic environment where stock prices fluctuate based on supply and demand. For example, if a company announces strong earnings, demand for its stock may surge, pushing its price higher. Conversely, negative news can trigger a sell-off, leading to a decline in stock prices.

For new investors, understanding how the stock market operates is vital. The market is divided into two primary segments: the primary market and the secondary market. The primary market is where new securities are issued, while the secondary market is where existing securities are traded. This distinction is significant as it illustrates the flow of capital within the economy. In the primary market, companies secure funds to finance operations, expand, or pay off debts. Meanwhile, the secondary market allows investors to buy and sell shares, providing liquidity and enabling price discovery—the process of determining a stock's fair value based on market conditions.

Furthermore, various factors influence the stock market, including economic indicators, interest rates, and geopolitical events. For instance, decisions made by the Federal Reserve regarding interest rates can have a profound impact on stock prices. When interest rates rise, borrowing costs increase, potentially slowing economic growth and adversely affecting corporate profits. On the other hand, lower interest rates can stimulate investment and consumer spending, resulting in higher stock prices. Recognizing these relationships empowers investors to make informed decisions about when to buy or sell stocks.

As we delve deeper into this chapter, we will explore how companies raise capital through IPOs and the intricacies of stock trading on major exchanges like the NYSE, NASDAQ and NSE. Additionally, we will examine various types of markets beyond stocks, including derivatives, forex, and commodities, providing a comprehensive overview of the financial landscape. By demystifying the stock market, this chapter aims to equip readers with the foundational knowledge necessary to engage confidently with financial markets.

In summary, the stock market is more than just a collection of numbers and charts; it is a vibrant ecosystem connecting companies seeking capital with investors aiming to grow their wealth. By understanding the fundamental concepts of stocks, exchanges, and market dynamics, readers will be better prepared to navigate the complexities of investing. As we progress through this chapter, we will build upon this foundation, exploring how companies raise capital and the various exchanges that facilitate stock trading, ultimately empowering readers to make informed investment decisions.

1.2 How Companies Raise Capital

In the dynamic world of business, companies constantly seek capital to fuel their growth, foster innovation, and expand their operations. This quest for funding propels them to explore various avenues for raising capital, each presenting unique advantages and challenges. One of the most significant methods employed is the Initial Public Offering (IPO), which allows companies to sell shares to the public for the first time. For new investors, grasping the intricacies of this process is essential, as it serves as a foundation for evaluating future investment opportunities.

An IPO represents a pivotal moment for a company, signifying its shift from private to public ownership. The journey begins when a company collaborates with investment banks to underwrite the offering. These banks play a crucial role in determining the initial share price, analyzing market conditions, and devising marketing strategies to attract potential investors. According to a report by Renaissance Capital, the average IPO in 2023 raised around $180 million, showcasing robust investor interest in newly public companies. This influx of capital empowers companies to invest in research and development, reduce debt, or venture into new markets.

However, the path to going public is fraught with risks. The IPO process demands rigorous regulatory compliance, including the submission of a registration statement to the Securities and Exchange Commission (SEC). This document offers comprehensive insights into the company's financial health, business model, and the risks associated with investing in its shares. The scrutiny involved can be overwhelming, and any negative perceptions can adversely impact the stock's performance post-IPO. A notable example is the 2022 IPO of Rivian Automotive, which initially generated excitement but saw its stock price plummet shortly thereafter due to production delays and broader market concerns.

Investors must also consider how an IPO affects a company's governance structure. Once a company becomes public, it is accountable to its shareholders, which can shift its focus from long-term growth strategies to short-term profit maximization. This shift can influence decision-making processes and may lead to conflicts between management and shareholders. For instance, WeWork faced intense scrutiny over its governance practices, ultimately contributing to its failed IPO attempt in 2019.

Beyond IPOs, companies have several alternative avenues for raising capital. Private placements involve selling securities directly to a select group of investors, often institutional ones, without the need for public registration. This method can be faster and less costly than an IPO, allowing companies to access funds while retaining greater control over their operations. According to PitchBook, private equity investments reached a record high of $1.2 trillion in 2023, underscoring the growing interest in private placements as a viable funding option.

Debt financing is another prevalent method, where companies issue bonds or secure loans to raise capital. This approach enables firms to maintain ownership while accessing necessary funds. However, it also creates an obligation to repay the borrowed amount along with interest, which can strain cash flow if not managed effectively. In 2023, corporate bond issuance totaled $1.5 trillion, reflecting the ongoing reliance on debt as a means of financing growth.

For new investors, understanding these various methods of capital raising is crucial. Each approach carries distinct implications for a company's financial health and growth trajectory. By analyzing how a company chooses to finance its operations, investors can glean insights into its strategic priorities and risk profile. For example, a company heavily reliant on debt may face heightened financial risk, particularly in a rising interest rate environment.

As we delve deeper into the stock market, it is essential to recognize how these capital-raising methods influence stock performance and investor sentiment. The next subchapter will examine major stock exchanges, such as the NYSE and NASDAQ, where these newly public companies trade their shares. Understanding the dynamics of these exchanges will further equip investors with the knowledge needed to navigate the complexities of the stock market effectively. What factors influence a stock's performance once it hits the exchange? How do trading mechanisms differ across platforms? These questions will guide our exploration in the upcoming section, enhancing your understanding of the broader financial landscape.

1.3 Major Stock Exchanges Explained

The stock market is a dynamic arena where companies seek to raise capital and investors engage in buying and selling shares. This chapter builds on the foundational concepts introduced earlier, such as Initial Public Offerings (IPOs) and the overall structure of the stock market. Now, we will delve into the major stock exchanges that facilitate these transactions: the New York Stock Exchange (NYSE), the National Association of Securities Dealers Automated Quotations (NASDAQ), and the National Stock Exchange of India (NSE). For new investors, understanding these exchanges is crucial, as each has distinct characteristics that shape trading practices and investment strategies.

The NYSE, founded in 1792, stands as one of the oldest and largest stock exchanges globally. It functions as an auction market, where buyers and sellers interact through designated market makers.

The NYSE enforces strict listing requirements, including minimum market capitalization and a specified number of publicly traded shares, ensuring that only established companies are listed. As of December 2024, the NYSE hosts over 2,100 companies, including industry giants like Apple and Microsoft, solidifying its role as a central hub for global finance.

In contrast, the NASDAQ, which began operations in 1971, operates as a dealer's market, facilitating transactions electronically rather than through physical trading floors. This exchange is particularly known for its technology-focused listings, attracting high-growth companies such as Amazon and Google. The NASDAQ has less stringent listing requirements compared to the NYSE, making it easier for smaller and newer companies to access public capital. By late 2024, the NASDAQ comprises approximately 3,800 companies, highlighting its appeal to tech-savvy investors.

The NSE, established in 1992, is India's leading stock exchange and plays a vital role in the country's financial ecosystem. Like the NASDAQ, the NSE operates electronically, providing a platform for trading various securities, including equities, derivatives, and debt instruments. Its robust regulatory framework and technological advancements have attracted both domestic and international investors. As of December 2024, the NSE lists over 2,600 companies, significantly contributing to India's economic growth.

While the NYSE, NASDAQ, and NSE share similar purposes, their operational mechanisms and market structures exhibit notable differences. The NYSE's auction model promotes transparency and price discovery, whereas the NASDAQ's electronic trading system enables faster transactions and greater accessibility. The NSE's emphasis on technology and innovation positions it as a key player in emerging markets. Understanding these distinctions empowers investors to make informed decisions about capital allocation based on their investment goals and risk tolerance.

Additionally, the trading hours and mechanisms of these exchanges vary. The NYSE operates from 9:30 AM to 4:00 PM Eastern Time, with options for pre-market and after-hours trading. The NASDAQ shares similar hours but offers more extensive after-hours trading opportunities. In contrast, the NSE operates from 9:15 AM to 3:30 PM Indian Standard Time, catering to local market needs. These timeframes can significantly influence trading strategies, especially for investors aiming to capitalize on short-term price movements.

Another critical aspect to consider is the role of indices associated with these exchanges. The NYSE features the Dow Jones Industrial Average (DJIA) and the S&P 500, while the NASDAQ includes the NASDAQ Composite Index. The NSE has its own benchmark indices, such as the Nifty 50 and the Sensex. These indices serve as vital indicators of market performance and are widely utilized by investors to assess the overall health of the stock market.

In conclusion, gaining familiarity with the major stock exchanges is an essential step for any aspiring investor. The NYSE, NASDAQ, and NSE each present unique opportunities and challenges shaped by their operational structures, listing requirements, and market dynamics. By understanding these exchanges, investors can navigate the complexities of the stock market more effectively and position themselves for success. As we move into the next chapter, we will explore various types of financial markets beyond stocks, further enhancing your investment knowledge and capabilities.

2

Types of Financial Markets

2.1 Primary vs. Secondary Markets

Grasping the differences between primary and secondary markets is essential for anyone aiming to navigate the stock market successfully. These two markets form the foundation of financial trading, each fulfilling a distinct role in the economy. The primary market is where new securities are created, enabling companies to raise capital by selling shares to investors for the first time. Conversely, the secondary market is where these existing securities are exchanged among investors, facilitating liquidity and price discovery. By understanding the functions of both markets, investors can make informed choices that align with their financial objectives.

The primary market operates through mechanisms such as Initial Public Offerings (IPOs), during which companies present shares to the public for the first time. This process not only aids businesses in securing funds for growth but also allows investors to become part- owners of a company right from its inception. A report by the Securities and Exchange Commission (SEC) in 2023 indicated that IPOs raised over $80 billion in the United States alone, underscoring the significance of this market in fostering corporate development and innovation.

Once securities are issued in the primary market, they transition to the secondary market, where investors can buy and sell them. This market is crucial for several reasons. First, it provides liquidity, allowing investors to quickly convert their holdings into cash. A study published in the Journal of Financial Economics in 2023 found that increased liquidity in the secondary market correlates with heightened investor confidence and participation. This liquidity is vital for maintaining an efficient market, as it enables smooth ownership transfers without substantial price fluctuations.

Another key function of the secondary market is price discovery, which involves determining the fair value of a security based on supply and demand dynamics. As investors engage in buying and selling shares, they contribute to the price formation of those securities. The continuous trading activity reflects collective sentiment regarding a company's future prospects, influenced by factors such as earnings reports, economic indicators, and market trends. According to a 2024 analysis by the Financial Industry Regulatory Authority (FINRA), effective price discovery mechanisms in the secondary market lead to more accurate valuations, essential for making well-informed investment decisions.

Furthermore, the secondary market plays a pivotal role in enhancing market efficiency. Efficient markets are characterized by the swift incorporation of new information into security prices. This efficiency is largely driven by the actions of various market participants, including institutional investors, retail traders, and market makers. For example, a 2023 report from the International Organization of Securities Commissions (IOSCO) highlighted that active participation in the secondary market helps ensure that prices reflect all available information, thereby minimizing the risk of mispricing.

Investors should also familiarize themselves with the different types of secondary markets, which include organized exchanges like the New York Stock Exchange (NYSE) and over-the-counter (OTC) markets. Organized exchanges offer a regulated environment for trading, while OTC markets facilitate transactions directly between parties, often with less transparency. Understanding these distinctions can assist investors in selecting the appropriate platform for their trading needs.

As we explore the complexities of financial markets in the upcoming sections, it is vital to recognize how the primary and secondary markets interconnect. The health of the primary market often mirrors the overall economic climate, while the secondary market provides the necessary infrastructure for ongoing trading and investment. By comprehending these relationships, investors can better position themselves to seize opportunities and manage risks effectively.

In summary, the primary and secondary markets are fundamental components of the financial ecosystem, each serving distinct yet interconnected purposes. The primary market facilitates capital formation for companies, while the secondary market ensures liquidity and efficient price discovery for investors. As we continue our exploration of financial markets, we will examine other types of markets, including derivatives and forex, which further enrich the landscape of investment opportunities. Understanding these markets will empower you to make informed decisions and navigate the complexities of investing with confidence.

2.2 Overview of Derivatives and Forex

Derivatives and forex markets are vital elements of the financial ecosystem, offering crucial tools for managing risk and facilitating currency exchange. As we build on our understanding of stock markets, it is essential to grasp how these markets function and their broader economic significance. This subchapter will introduce derivatives, including futures and options, and explore the forex market, emphasizing its global scope and the various factors that affect currency values.

Derivatives are financial instruments whose value is linked to an underlying asset, such as stocks, bonds, commodities, or currencies. They serve multiple purposes, primarily allowing investors to hedge against price fluctuations or speculate on future price movements. According to the Bank for International Settlements (BIS), the notional amount of outstanding derivatives contracts reached approximately $640 trillion in 2022, highlighting their extensive use in financial markets (BIS, 2023).

Futures contracts represent one of the most prevalent types of derivatives. These agreements require the buyer to purchase, and the seller to sell, an asset at a predetermined price on a specified future date. Futures are commonly utilized in commodities markets, enabling producers and consumers to secure prices and reduce the risk of price volatility. For example, a farmer might enter into a futures contract to sell their crop at a fixed price, thereby safeguarding against potential declines in market prices at harvest time.

Options constitute another important category of derivatives, providing the holder with the right, but not the obligation, to buy or sell an underlying asset at a specified price before a designated date. There are two main types of options: call options, which confer the right to buy, and put options, which grant the right to sell. Options can be used for both hedging and speculative trading. A recent study by the Options Clearing Corporation revealed that the average daily volume of options traded in 2023 was around 40 million contracts, indicating their popularity among investors (OCC, 2023).

Grasping the mechanics of derivatives is crucial for investors interested in advanced trading strategies. By employing futures and options, investors can effectively manage risks associated with price fluctuations, enhancing their ability to navigate volatile markets. This knowledge becomes particularly relevant as we turn our attention to the forex market, which operates on a global scale and is influenced by numerous factors.

The foreign exchange (forex) market stands as the largest and most liquid financial market globally, boasting an average daily trading volume exceeding $6 trillion as of 2023 (Bank for International Settlements, 2023). Unlike stock markets, which are centralized, the forex market functions over-the-counter (OTC), meaning transactions occur directly between parties, typically through electronic trading platforms. This decentralized structure allows for continuous trading across different time zones, making the forex market accessible to investors worldwide.

Currency values in the forex market are shaped by a variety of factors, including interest rates, economic indicators, geopolitical events, and market sentiment. For instance, when a country's central bank raises interest rates, it often leads to an appreciation of its currency, as higher rates attract foreign capital seeking better returns. Conversely, political instability or economic downturns can lead to currency depreciation, as investors gravitate toward safer assets. Understanding these dynamics is essential for investors looking to engage in forex trading or hedge against currency risk.

Furthermore, the forex market is distinguished by its unique terminology and trading strategies. Currency pairs, such as EUR/USD or USD/JPY, reflect the value of one currency relative to another. Traders can adopt various strategies, including scalping, day trading, and swing trading, each with its own risk-reward profile. According to a report by the Financial Conduct Authority, approximately 75% of retail forex traders incur losses, underscoring the importance of risk management and education in this highly competitive environment (FCA, 2023).

In conclusion, recognizing the roles of derivatives and forex in the broader financial ecosystem is essential. Both markets provide valuable mechanisms for managing risk and facilitating international trade. With a solid grasp of these concepts, readers will be better equipped to explore more advanced trading strategies in the subsequent subchapter, where we will delve into cryptocurrency markets and their implications for investors.

2.3 Introduction to Cryptocurrency Markets

The rise of cryptocurrency markets marks a transformative shift in the financial landscape, presenting both exciting opportunities and notable challenges for investors. As we move away from traditional stock markets and embrace these digital platforms, it becomes crucial to grasp how cryptocurrency markets function, the technology that drives them, and the implications for investment strategies.

At the heart of cryptocurrency markets is blockchain technology, a decentralized ledger system that securely records transactions across numerous computers. This innovative technology fosters transparency and security, making it exceedingly difficult for any single entity to alter the data. A 2023 report from the World Economic Forum projects that blockchain technology will underpin 10% of global GDP by 2027, underscoring its increasing significance across various sectors beyond finance.

Cryptocurrencies like Bitcoin and Ethereum serve as digital assets traded on numerous exchanges. Unlike traditional currencies, which are issued and regulated by central banks, cryptocurrencies operate independently, contributing to their inherent volatility. As of early 2023, the total market capitalization of cryptocurrencies reached approximately $2.5 trillion, reflecting a surge in interest from both retail and institutional investors. This growth has been fueled by factors such as heightened adoption, speculative trading, and the allure of substantial returns.

However, investing in cryptocurrency markets carries inherent risks. The volatility associated with cryptocurrencies can result in dramatic price swings over short periods. For example, Bitcoin saw its value plummet by over 50% in 2022, highlighting the unpredictable nature of these assets. Additionally, regulatory scrutiny is intensifying worldwide, with governments actively exploring frameworks to govern cryptocurrency transactions. A 2023 study by the Financial Stability Board revealed that 70% of countries are considering or have already implemented regulations concerning cryptocurrencies, which could significantly influence market dynamics and investor behavior.

For new investors, understanding the structure of cryptocurrency markets is essential. These markets operate around the clock, unlike traditional stock exchanges, facilitating continuous trading. Major cryptocurrency exchanges, such as Binance and Coinbase, enable the buying and selling of digital assets, providing liquidity and access to a diverse array of cryptocurrencies. Furthermore, decentralized finance (DeFi) platforms have emerged, allowing users to lend, borrow, and trade cryptocurrencies without intermediaries, thereby broadening the market's reach.

As we explore cryptocurrency markets further, it is vital to consider the various investment vehicles available. Investors can opt to buy and hold cryptocurrencies directly, trade them on exchanges, or invest in cryptocurrency-related funds and products. For instance, exchange- traded funds (ETFs) that track cryptocurrency performance have gained traction, offering a more conventional investment approach while still exposing investors to the crypto market's volatility.

Additionally, the emergence of non-fungible tokens (NFTs) has introduced another dimension to the cryptocurrency ecosystem. NFTs signify ownership of unique digital assets, such as art or collectibles, and have attracted considerable attention and investment. In 2022, the NFT market generated over $40 billion in sales, illustrating the potential for innovative investment opportunities within the broader cryptocurrency landscape.

In summary, the advent of cryptocurrency markets presents a complex yet thrilling opportunity for investors. By comprehending the foundational technology, market structure, and potential risks, investors can navigate this evolving landscape more effectively. As we prepare to delve into specific investment vehicles in the next chapter, staying informed about ongoing developments in the cryptocurrency space is paramount. The rapid evolution of this market highlights the necessity for adaptability and continuous learning to achieve successful investing.

3

Investment Vehicles Explained

3.1 Stocks, Bonds, and ETFs Defined

Embarking on your investment journey requires a solid understanding of the key vehicles at your disposal. Stocks, bonds, and exchange-traded funds (ETFs) are foundational components of many investment portfolios, each offering distinct characteristics, risk profiles, and potential returns. By familiarizing yourself with these essential concepts, you will be better positioned to develop an investment strategy that aligns with your financial aspirations and risk tolerance.

Stocks signify ownership in a company. When you acquire a stock, you purchase a share of that company, granting you a claim on its assets and earnings. Stocks are traded on exchanges such as the New York Stock Exchange (NYSE) and NASDAQ, where their prices fluctuate based on supply and demand. Historically, stocks have yielded higher returns than other asset classes, averaging around 10% annually over the long term, according to data from the Ibbotson Associates study (2023). However, this potential for substantial returns is accompanied by increased volatility, making stocks more suitable for investors who can withstand short-term price fluctuations.

Bonds, in contrast, are debt instruments issued by corporations or governments to raise capital. When you purchase a bond, you are effectively lending money to the issuer in exchange for periodic interest payments and the return of the bond's face value upon maturity. Generally regarded as safer than stocks, bonds provide fixed income and are less vulnerable to market volatility. According to the Bloomberg Barclays Global Aggregate Bond Index, the average annual return for bonds has been approximately 5% over the past decade (2023). However, this lower risk typically translates to lower returns compared to stocks, making bonds more appealing to conservative investors or those seeking income stability.

Exchange-traded funds (ETFs) blend features of both stocks and mutual funds. An ETF is a collection of securities—such as stocks or bonds—that trades on an exchange like a stock. This structure allows investors to buy shares of the ETF, which represents a diversified portfolio of assets. One of the primary advantages of ETFs is their liquidity; they can be bought and sold throughout the trading day at market prices. Furthermore, ETFs often boast lower expense ratios compared to mutual funds, making them a cost-effective choice for investors. According to Morningstar (2023), the average expense ratio for ETFs is around 0.44%, compared to 0.74% for mutual funds. However, similar to stocks, ETFs can also experience price volatility, influenced by the performance of the underlying assets.

Grasping the risk profiles associated with these investment vehicles is vital for crafting a well-rounded investment strategy. Stocks offer the potential for significant growth but come with the risk of price fluctuations and possible losses. Bonds deliver a more stable income stream, although they may not keep pace with inflation over time. ETFs provide diversification and flexibility, yet their performance is closely tied to the market conditions of the underlying assets.

As you evaluate your investment options, it is crucial to reflect on your individual preferences and financial objectives. Are you seeking growth, income, or a combination of both? Your responses to these questions will guide your decisions regarding the allocation of your investment portfolio among stocks, bonds, and ETFs. For example, younger investors with a longer time horizon may favor stocks for growth, while those approaching retirement might prioritize bonds for income stability.

This subchapter has established a foundation for understanding the three primary investment vehicles: stocks, bonds, and ETFs. Each possesses its own set of characteristics, risks, and rewards, all of which can significantly influence your investment strategy. In the next subchapter, we will explore mutual funds and Real Estate Investment Trusts (REITs), examining how these additional investment options can further diversify your portfolio and enhance your financial growth. By expanding your knowledge of various investment vehicles, you will be better equipped to navigate the complexities of the financial markets and make informed decisions that align with your goals.

3.2 Understanding Mutual Funds and REITs

As we explore the landscape of investment vehicles, it's crucial to revisit the concept of diversification, a strategy introduced in the previous subchapter. Diversification is essential for managing risk, as it involves spreading investments across various asset classes. Two prominent options for achieving this are mutual funds and Real Estate Investment Trusts (REITs). These investment vehicles offer unique opportunities for investors to create diversified portfolios without requiring extensive expertise or direct management of individual assets.

Mutual funds are investment programs funded by shareholders and professionally managed to trade in diversified holdings. They aggregate capital from multiple investors to form a single fund that invests in a broad spectrum of securities, including stocks, bonds, and other assets. According to the Investment Company Institute (ICI), mutual funds held approximately $23 trillion in assets in the United States as of mid-2023, underscoring their popularity among investors seeking both diversification and professional management (ICI, 2023).

A key advantage of mutual funds is their capacity to provide instant diversification. When an investor puts money into a mutual fund, they gain exposure to a wide range of securities, which can lessen the impact of poor performance from any single investment. For instance, if a mutual fund includes shares from 100 different companies, the underperformance of one company is unlikely to significantly affect the overall value of the fund. This feature is particularly attractive to novice investors who may lack the time or expertise to research and select individual stocks.

Furthermore, mutual funds are overseen by professional portfolio managers who make investment decisions on behalf of the investors. These managers conduct comprehensive research and analysis to choose securities that align with the fund's investment objectives. This level of professional oversight can be advantageous for those who prefer a more hands-off approach to investing. However, it's important to note that mutual funds typically charge management fees, which can vary widely based on the fund's structure and performance.

On the other hand, Real Estate Investment Trusts (REITs) present a distinct avenue for diversification, enabling investors to gain exposure to real estate markets without the complexities of direct property ownership. A REIT is a company that owns, operates, or finances income-generating real estate across various property sectors. As reported by the National Association of Real Estate Investment Trusts (NAREIT), the U.S. REIT market was valued at approximately $1.5 trillion in 2023, highlighting its significance as an investment vehicle (NAREIT, 2023).

Investing in REITs offers several benefits. Primarily, they provide a means to invest in real estate without the burdens of property management. Investors can purchase shares of publicly traded REITs on major stock exchanges, similar to buying stocks. This liquidity is a considerable advantage over traditional real estate investments, which often require substantial capital and involve lengthy transaction processes.

Additionally, REITs are legally obligated to distribute at least 90% of their taxable income to shareholders in the form of dividends. This requirement makes them an appealing option for income-seeking investors. As of 2023, the average dividend yield for equity REITs was around 4%, offering a steady income stream for investors (NAREIT,

2023). However, like mutual funds, REITs also carry risks, including market volatility and the potential for fluctuating property values.

Both mutual funds and REITs are effective tools for diversifying an investment portfolio. While mutual funds allow investors to access a variety of asset classes through a single investment, REITs provide a unique opportunity to invest in real estate without the challenges of direct ownership. As investors weigh their options, it is vital to assess their financial goals, risk tolerance, and investment horizon.

In conclusion, mutual funds and REITs are valuable investment vehicles that can enhance portfolio diversification. They cater to different investment preferences and objectives, making them suitable for a wide array of investors. As we move to the next subchapter, we will examine how to compare these investment options with others, such as stocks and bonds, to make informed decisions that align with individual financial goals. Understanding the nuances of each investment type will empower readers to navigate the complexities of the financial markets with confidence.

3.3 Comparing Investment Options

As we wrap up our examination of various investment vehicles, it's essential to distill the insights we've gathered. We've explored stocks, bonds, ETFs, mutual funds, and REITs, each presenting distinct characteristics, benefits, and drawbacks. Grasping these differences is vital for making informed investment choices that resonate with your financial aspirations and risk appetite.

Stocks signify ownership in a company and can yield substantial returns through capital appreciation and dividends. However, they also entail higher volatility and risk, especially in the short term. A 2023 report from S&P Dow Jones Indices indicates that the average annual return of the S&P 500 over the past 90 years has been around 10%. This figure, however, conceals periods of significant fluctuation. Thus, while stocks can be a potent means of wealth accumulation, they necessitate a long-term outlook and a readiness to weather market fluctuations.

Bonds, conversely, are typically viewed as safer investments compared to stocks. They offer fixed interest payments and return the principal at maturity, making them appealing to conservative investors seeking stability. The Bloomberg Barclays U.S. Aggregate Bond Index reported an average annual return of approximately 4.5% over the last decade, underscoring their role as a stabilizing element in a diversified portfolio. Nevertheless, bonds carry risks; fluctuations in interest rates can impact bond prices, and inflation may diminish purchasing power over time.

Exchange-Traded Funds (ETFs) blend the diversification advantages of mutual funds with the trading flexibility of stocks. Generally, they feature lower expense ratios than mutual funds and can be traded throughout the day like individual stocks. According to Morningstar, as of 2023, the average expense ratio for ETFs was 0.44%, compared to 0.74% for mutual funds. This cost-effectiveness makes ETFs an attractive choice for many investors. However, it's essential to remain mindful of potential liquidity issues and the influence of trading costs on overall returns.

Mutual funds present another avenue for diversification, pooling resources from multiple investors to invest in a wide array of assets. Managed by professionals, they can be advantageous for those who prefer a more hands-off approach. However, mutual funds often come with higher fees and may impose restrictions on buying and selling, rendering them less flexible than ETFs. The Investment Company Institute noted that the average expense ratio for actively managed mutual funds was 0.74% in 2023, highlighting the importance of scrutinizing costs when selecting funds.

Real Estate Investment Trusts (REITs) offer exposure to real estate markets without the necessity of direct property ownership. They can provide appealing dividend yields and potential for capital appreciation. The National Association of Real Estate Investment Trusts reported that the average annual total return for REITs was about 9.6% over the past 20 years. However, investing in REITs carries risks, including market volatility and sensitivity to interest rates, which can affect property values and rental income.

When evaluating these investment options, it is crucial to reflect on your personal financial situation, investment objectives, and risk tolerance. A well-diversified portfolio might encompass a mix of stocks, bonds, ETFs, mutual funds, and REITs, allowing you to balance potential returns with effective risk management. As highlighted by the CFA Institute in 2023, diversification remains one of the most effective strategies for mitigating risk in investment portfolios.

Additionally, being aware of the current market environment and economic indicators can further guide your investment decisions. For example, rising interest rates may favor bonds over stocks, while a robust economy could enhance stock performance. Staying informed about these trends will empower you to make timely adjustments to your portfolio.

In summary, the comparative analysis of investment vehicles presented in this chapter lays the groundwork for your investment journey. Each option possesses its own set of advantages and disadvantages, and the optimal choice hinges on your individual circumstances and goals. As we move to the next chapter, where we will discuss how to open a brokerage account, remember that the knowledge you've acquired here will be instrumental in shaping your investment decisions moving forward. By comprehending the nuances of each investment vehicle, you will be better equipped to navigate the complexities of the stock market and embark on a successful investment journey.

4

Opening a Brokerage Account

4.1 Choosing the Right Brokerage

Embarking on your investment journey in the stock market begins with a pivotal choice: selecting the right brokerage. This decision can profoundly shape your investment experience and significantly impact your ability to build wealth. With a plethora of options available, each presenting unique features, fees, and services, navigating this terrain can feel overwhelming, especially for newcomers. However, by grasping the essential factors to consider when choosing a brokerage, you can make an informed decision that aligns with your financial aspirations.

At its essence, a brokerage serves as the bridge between you and the stock market, enabling the buying and selling of securities. The type of brokerage you opt for can influence everything from trading costs to the tools and resources at your disposal. Thus, it is crucial to assess several key criteria before making your choice.

One of the foremost considerations is the brokerage's fee structure. Brokerages impose various fees, including trade commissions, account maintenance charges, and fees for premium services. A 2023 report from the Financial Industry Regulatory Authority (FINRA) indicates that average commissions for online trades have significantly decreased over the past decade, with many brokerages now offering commission- free trading on stocks and ETFs. Nevertheless, it is vital to scrutinize the fine print, as some brokerages may levy higher fees for other services or include hidden costs that could affect your overall returns.

Beyond fees, the range of services provided by a brokerage is another critical factor. Some brokerages offer a comprehensive suite of tools, including research reports, educational resources, and advanced trading platforms, while others may adopt a more streamlined approach. For beginners eager to learn, a brokerage that provides extensive educational materials and user-friendly interfaces can greatly enhance the investing experience. In contrast, seasoned investors might prioritize access to sophisticated trading tools and analytics. A 2024 survey by J.D. Power revealed that 75% of investors consider educational resources a key factor in their brokerage selection, underscoring the importance of aligning your choice with your expertise level.

User experience is equally important when evaluating a brokerage. A well-designed platform can significantly ease the process of executing trades and managing investments. Seek brokerages that offer intuitive mobile and web applications, allowing you to trade on the go and access your portfolio whenever needed. Additionally, assess the quality of customer support available. During times of uncertainty or technical issues, having responsive and knowledgeable support can alleviate stress and enhance your overall experience.

Moreover, consider the types of accounts offered by the brokerage. Many brokerages provide various account types, including individual, joint, retirement, and custodial accounts. Each account type comes with distinct features and benefits, so it is essential to select one that aligns with your investment strategy and long-term objectives. For instance, if you are planning for retirement, a brokerage specializing in retirement accounts may offer valuable tax advantages and investment options tailored to your needs.

As you evaluate these factors, it is also wise to read reviews and seek recommendations from fellow investors. Online forums, social media groups, and financial news websites can offer insights into the experiences of other users, helping you assess the reliability and reputation of potential brokerages. Remember, the goal is to find a brokerage that not only meets your immediate needs but also fosters your growth as an investor over time.

In conclusion, selecting the right brokerage is a foundational step in your investment journey. By thoughtfully considering factors such as fees, services offered, user experience, and account types, you can choose a brokerage that aligns with your financial goals and enhances your investing experience. As we progress in this chapter, we will delve into the different types of brokerage accounts available, equipping you with the knowledge necessary to maximize your chosen platform. Understanding these distinctions will empower you to confidently take the next steps in your investment journey.

4.2 Types of Brokerage Accounts

Understanding the pivotal role of brokerage firms in the stock market is just the beginning; it's equally important to familiarize yourself with the different types of brokerage accounts available to investors. Choosing the right account type is a critical step in your investment journey, as each account serves distinct purposes and comes with unique features tailored to various financial goals.

The most prevalent type of brokerage account is the individual account. This account is opened by a single investor, allowing them to buy and sell securities under their name. Individual accounts grant complete control over investment decisions, enabling investors to customize their portfolios based on personal risk tolerance and financial objectives. A 2023 report from the Financial Industry Regulatory Authority (FINRA) indicates that individual accounts make up approximately 70% of all brokerage accounts in the United States, underscoring their popularity among retail investors. Similarly in India The National Stock Exchange (NSE) reported over 11 crore (110 million) unique registered investors by January 2025, highlighting a significant increase in direct stock market participation

In contrast, a joint brokerage account is intended for two or more individuals who wish to invest collaboratively. Often utilized by couples or business partners, this account allows shared investment responsibilities and decision-making. Joint accounts can be structured as either joint tenants with rights of survivorship or tenants in common, which influences how assets are distributed upon the death of one account holder. A 2023 survey conducted by Charles Schwab revealed that nearly 25% of investors preferred joint accounts for collaborative investing, highlighting the significance of shared financial goals in partnerships.

Retirement accounts represent another essential category, encompassing options such as Individual Retirement Accounts (IRAs) and 401(k) plans. These accounts are specifically designed to promote long-term savings for retirement. Contributions to traditional IRAs may be tax-deductible, with investments growing tax-deferred until withdrawal. Conversely, Roth IRAs allow for tax-free growth and withdrawals during retirement. According to the Investment Company Institute, over 50 million Americans held IRAs as of 2023, reflecting an increasing awareness of the importance of retirement planning. Understanding the tax implications and contribution limits of these accounts is crucial for maximizing retirement savings.

For those interested in investing on behalf of minors, custodial accounts provide a viable solution. Established by an adult for a minor, these accounts enable the adult to manage investments until the child reaches the age of majority, typically 18 or 21, depending on state laws. Custodial accounts serve as a valuable tool for teaching children about investing and saving, offering a hands-on approach to financial education. Governed by the Uniform Transfers to Minors Act (UTMA), these accounts ensure that assets are used for the benefit of the minor.

Each type of brokerage account presents its own advantages and disadvantages. Individual accounts offer flexibility and control, while joint accounts encourage collaboration and shared investment strategies. Retirement accounts provide tax benefits and promote long-term savings, and custodial accounts facilitate early financial education for minors. When considering which account type best aligns with your financial situation, it is essential to assess your investment goals, time horizon, and desired level of involvement in managing your investments.

Furthermore, understanding the fees associated with each account type is vital. Brokerage firms may impose account maintenance fees, trading commissions, or management fees, all of which can impact your overall investment returns. A 2023 report from the Securities and Exchange Commission (SEC) emphasized the importance of carefully reviewing fee structures when selecting a brokerage account, as even minor differences in fees can significantly affect long-term investment growth.

As you explore the various brokerage account options, keep in mind that your choice will influence your investment strategy and overall financial success. Conducting thorough research and possibly consulting with a financial advisor can help ensure that your selected account type aligns with your financial objectives.

With a solid grasp of the different types of brokerage accounts available, you are now better prepared to take the next step in your investment journey. In the following subchapter, we will guide you through the process of setting up your brokerage account, providing a step-by-step approach to navigate this essential phase of investing. By clarifying the account opening process, we aim to empower you to take action and embark on your investment endeavors with confidence.

4.3 Setting Up Your Account

After selecting a brokerage that aligns with your investment goals, the next important step is to set up your account. While this process may initially appear overwhelming, breaking it down into manageable steps can ease your entry into the stock market. In this section, we will guide you through the account opening process, detailing the necessary documentation and initial funding, so you can confidently take actionable steps toward investing.

Understanding the types of accounts available is essential. Most brokerages provide individual accounts, joint accounts, retirement accounts (such as IRAs), and custodial accounts for minors. Each account type serves distinct purposes and comes with unique tax implications. For example, a traditional IRA allows for tax-deferred growth, while a Roth IRA offers tax-free withdrawals during retirement. Choosing the right account type is crucial, as it can significantly influence your investment strategy and tax responsibilities.

Once you have identified the appropriate account type, the next step is to gather the required documentation. Typically, brokerages will request personal identification information, including your Social Security number, driver's license or passport, and proof of address (such as a utility bill) or AADHAR card for India. According to the Financial Industry Regulatory Authority (FINRA), these documents are necessary to comply with federal regulations designed to prevent fraud and protect your investments (FINRA, 2023). Additionally, be prepared to provide your employment details and financial background, as this information helps the brokerage evaluate your investment experience and risk tolerance.

With your documentation in hand, you can begin the application process. Most brokerages offer an online application that is user-friendly and straightforward. During this process, you will create a username and password, set security questions, and review the brokerage's terms and conditions. It is vital to read these documents carefully, as they outline the fees, services, and policies governing your account. A 2023 survey by J.D. Power revealed that nearly 60% of investors indicated that understanding fee structures significantly influenced their choice of brokerage (J.D. Power, 2023).

After submitting your application, the brokerage will review your information, which usually takes anywhere from a few minutes to a few days. If approved, you will receive an email confirmation along with instructions on how to fund your account. Initial funding is a critical step, as it activates your account and enables you to start trading. Most brokerages provide various funding options, including bank transfers, wire transfers, and checks. Familiarizing yourself with the available funding methods is advisable, as some may incur fees or experience processing delays.

When funding your account, consider starting with an amount you are comfortable investing. Many experts suggest beginning with a sum that allows you to explore different investment strategies without risking significant capital. A 2023 report from Charles Schwab recommends that new investors aim to invest at least $1,000 to effectively diversify their portfolios (Charles Schwab, 2023). This amount enables you to purchase multiple stocks or ETFs, thereby reducing the risk associated with individual investments.

Once your account is funded, you will gain access to the brokerage's trading platform. Familiarizing yourself with this platform is essential, as it will serve as your primary tool for executing trades and managing your investments. Most platforms offer educational resources, including tutorials and webinars, to help you navigate their features. Engaging with these resources can enhance your understanding of the tools available, empowering you to make informed decisions in the market.

In summary, setting up your brokerage account is a crucial step in your investment journey. By understanding the types of accounts available, gathering the necessary documentation, and following the application process, you can confidently establish your presence in the stock market. This foundational knowledge not only prepares you for investing but also sets the stage for the next chapter, where we will explore how to place orders in the market. As you embark on this exciting venture, remember that preparation and education are key to becoming a successful investor.

5

Placing Orders in the Market

5.1 Market Orders vs. Limit Orders

Navigating the stock market requires a solid understanding of how to execute trades effectively. Among the various methods available, market orders and limit orders are the two primary types that investors can utilize to buy or sell stocks. Each order type possesses distinct characteristics, advantages, and disadvantages that can significantly influence trading outcomes. By comprehending the differences between these orders, investors can refine their trading strategies and enhance their overall investment experience.

A market order is the most straightforward type of order, directing a broker to buy or sell a stock immediately at the best available price. This order type is particularly beneficial when speed is of the essence, such as during rapid market fluctuations or when trading highly liquid stocks. A 2023 report from the Financial Industry Regulatory Authority (FINRA) indicates that market orders constituted approximately 70% of all equity trades executed on major exchanges, highlighting their popularity among investors who prioritize immediate execution.

However, while market orders facilitate quick execution, they carry inherent risks. The most notable drawback is the potential for slippage, which occurs when the execution price deviates from the expected price due to market volatility. For example, if an investor places a market order to buy a stock at $50, but the price rises to $51 before the order is filled, the investor will end up paying the higher price. This issue can be especially pronounced in volatile markets or for stocks with lower trading volumes, where prices can change rapidly.

In contrast, a limit order empowers investors to set the maximum price they are willing to pay when buying or the minimum price they are willing to accept when selling. This order type offers greater control over the execution price, making it an appealing choice for those who prioritize price over speed. For instance, if an investor aims to purchase shares of a stock currently trading at $50 but anticipates a price drop, they might place a limit order at $48. If the stock reaches that price, the order will be executed; otherwise, it remains unfilled until the specified price is achieved.

Limit orders also help mitigate the risk of slippage, ensuring that investors do not pay more than their specified price when buying or receive less than their desired price when selling. A study published in the Journal of Finance in 2024 found that investors using limit orders experienced a 15% improvement in execution prices compared to those utilizing market orders during periods of high volatility. This advantage underscores the importance of employing limit orders under certain market conditions, particularly for risk-averse investors.

Despite their advantages, limit orders have their own limitations. A significant drawback is that they may not be executed at all if the market price does not reach the specified limit. This situation can be frustrating for investors who miss out on potential opportunities because their orders remain unfilled. Additionally, limit orders can result in partial fills, where only a portion of the order is executed at the limit price, leaving the investor with an incomplete position.

Understanding when to use each type of order is vital for optimizing trading strategies. Market orders are best suited for scenarios where immediate execution is crucial, such as during earnings announcements or significant news events that could impact stock prices. Conversely, limit orders are ideal for investors with specific price targets who are willing to wait for the market to meet those targets before executing their trades.

As investors become more acquainted with these order types, they can navigate the complexities of the stock market more effectively. In the upcoming sections, we will explore additional order types, such as stop-loss orders, which serve as essential tools for managing risk in trading. By broadening their understanding of order execution and timing, readers will be better equipped to make informed decisions and enhance their overall investment strategies.

5.2 Understanding Stop-Loss Orders

As we explore the intricacies of placing orders in the stock market, it is crucial to revisit the concept of risk management discussed earlier. While market and limit orders are essential tools for executing trades, stop-loss orders play a vital role in protecting investments from unexpected market shifts. By grasping how stop-loss orders operate, investors can better shield their portfolios from significant losses, ultimately strengthening their trading strategies.

A stop-loss order is a directive given to a broker to sell a security when its price hits a predetermined level, known as the stop price. This mechanism aims to limit an investor's potential loss on a security position. For example, if an investor buys shares of a company at $50 and sets a stop-loss order at $45, the broker will automatically sell the shares if the price drops to $45. This automatic execution helps reduce potential losses without necessitating constant market monitoring by the investor.

The true power of stop-loss orders lies in their ability to eliminate emotional decision-making from trading. A 2023 study by the CFA Institute revealed that nearly 60% of retail investors admitted that emotions like fear and greed heavily influenced their trading choices (CFA Institute, 2023). By utilizing stop-loss orders, investors can set predefined exit points, enabling them to stick to their trading plans even amid market volatility. For instance, a SEBI study revealed that 93% of individual traders in the equity derivatives segment incurred losses between FY22 and FY24.

There are various types of stop-loss orders, each designed for specific purposes. The most common is the standard stop-loss order, which triggers a market order once the stop price is reached. Investors might also consider a trailing stop-loss order, which adjusts the stop price by a fixed percentage or dollar amount below the market price as the security's price increases. For instance, if an investor sets a trailing stop- loss order at 10% below the current market price of a stock, the stop price will rise with the stock, securing profits while still offering downside protection.

Recent data highlights the significance of stop-loss orders in volatile markets. A Bloomberg report from 2024 indicated that technology sector stocks experienced an average daily price fluctuation of 3.5% during the first quarter, underscoring the need for effective risk management strategies (Bloomberg, 2024). In such unpredictable environments, stop-loss orders can be indispensable for investors aiming to safeguard their capital while navigating market uncertainties.

Integrating stop-loss strategies into a broader trading plan can significantly enhance an investor's risk management capabilities. However, it is essential to determine the appropriate stop price based on individual risk tolerance and prevailing market conditions. Setting a stop price too close to the current market price may lead to premature selling due to normal price fluctuations, while setting it too far away could expose the investor to larger losses. Thus, careful analysis and consideration are vital when establishing stop-loss levels.

Moreover, investors should be aware of the limitations associated with stop-loss orders. In fast-moving markets, a stop-loss order may not execute at the exact stop price due to slippage, which occurs when the market price surpasses the stop price before the order can be filled. This situation can result in greater losses than anticipated, especially in highly volatile conditions. Therefore, it is advisable for investors to complement stop-loss orders with other risk management techniques, such as diversification and position sizing, to create a more resilient investment strategy.

As we move to the next subchapter, it is important to recognize that while stop-loss orders are powerful tools for managing risk, they represent just one aspect of a comprehensive trading strategy.

Understanding the nuances of order execution and timing will further equip investors to navigate the complexities of the stock market. In the following section, we will examine how the timing of order execution can significantly influence investment outcomes, shedding light on the factors that determine when to enter or exit trades.

5.3 Order Execution and Timing

The timing of order execution is a crucial factor that can greatly influence investment outcomes. While understanding the different types of orders—market, limit, and stop-loss—is fundamental for effective trading, knowing when to execute these orders is equally important. This subchapter examines the various factors that affect order execution, such as market conditions and liquidity, and illustrates how these elements can guide your trading decisions.

Market conditions are essential in determining the best timing for order execution. In times of high volatility, prices can change rapidly within short periods. A 2023 report from the Financial Industry Regulatory Authority (FINRA) noted that stocks could experience price swings exceeding 5% in a single trading day during volatile conditions. This highlights the necessity of being aware of broader market trends and significant news events that can impact stock prices. For example, earnings reports, economic data releases, or geopolitical events can trigger sudden increases in volatility, making it vital for investors to remain informed and prepared to act swiftly.

Liquidity is another key factor influencing order execution. It refers to how easily an asset can be bought or sold in the market without significantly affecting its price. In highly liquid markets, such as those for large-cap stocks, orders can be executed quickly at desired prices. Conversely, in illiquid markets, order execution may take longer, and prices may shift unfavorably before the order is completed. A study published in the Journal of Finance in 2023 found that stocks with lower liquidity often exhibit larger spreads between bid and ask prices, which can diminish potential profits for investors. Therefore, understanding the liquidity of the assets you are trading is vital for optimizing your entry and exit points.

The time of day also plays a significant role in order execution. The stock market experiences varying levels of activity throughout the trading day. Typically, the opening and closing hours see the highest trading volumes, leading to faster execution times. In contrast, midday trading often experiences lower volumes, which can result in slower execution and less favorable pricing. A 2024 analysis by Bloomberg revealed that about 30% of daily trading volume occurs within the first hour after the market opens, underscoring the importance of strategically timing your trades.

When deciding when to place your orders, it is crucial to assess your trading strategy and objectives. Long-term investors may focus more on a company's fundamentals rather than short-term price fluctuations, allowing them to be less concerned about precise timing. In contrast, if you are pursuing short-term trading strategies, such as day trading or swing trading, precise timing becomes critical. In these situations, utilizing technical analysis tools like moving averages or momentum indicators can help pinpoint optimal entry and exit points based on historical price patterns.

Additionally, grasping the concept of slippage is essential for effective order execution. Slippage occurs when an order is filled at a different price than anticipated, often due to rapid market movements. A 2023 survey by the CFA Institute indicated that nearly 40% of traders experienced slippage in their transactions, highlighting the need for careful consideration of market conditions before placing orders. To minimize slippage, traders can employ limit orders, which specify the maximum price they are willing to pay or the minimum price they are willing to accept, thus providing greater control over execution prices.

In summary, the timing of order execution is a complex aspect of trading that necessitates careful evaluation of market conditions, liquidity, and individual trading strategies. By comprehending these dynamics, you can make more informed decisions regarding when to enter or exit trades, ultimately enhancing your trading effectiveness. As we move to the next chapter, which will explore the differences between investing and trading, remember that the principles of order execution and timing will remain integral to shaping your investment approach. Whether you opt for a long-term investment strategy or engage in short-term trading, mastering the art of timing is essential for achieving your financial goals.

6

Investing vs. Trading

6.1 Long-Term Investment Strategies

Investing in the stock market can be likened to embarking on a journey across an expansive ocean, where unpredictable waves and hidden currents abound. For newcomers, the idea of building wealth through long-term investment strategies may appear overwhelming. Yet, grasping the essentials of long-term investing can equip individuals with the confidence needed to navigate these turbulent waters. This approach centers on accumulating wealth over time through asset appreciation, anchored in principles that prioritize patience, diligent research, and strategic decision-making.

At its essence, long-term investing emphasizes that wealth accumulation is a gradual process rather than a quick race. A 2023 report from the Financial Industry Regulatory Authority (FINRA) reveals that investors who adopt a long-term outlook are more likely to meet their financial objectives compared to those who engage in short-term trading. This advantage arises because long-term investments can endure market volatility and harness the power of compounding returns over time. As Albert Einstein famously stated, "Compound interest is the eighth wonder of the world." This principle highlights the necessity of allowing investments to mature without the stress of seeking immediate returns.

Within the framework of long-term investing, two prominent strategies stand out: value investing and dividend investing. Value investing, championed by notable figures like Warren Buffett, involves pinpointing undervalued stocks with robust fundamentals.

The strategy entails acquiring these stocks at prices below their intrinsic value, anticipating that the market will eventually acknowledge their true worth. A 2023 study by the CFA Institute demonstrated that value stocks outperformed growth stocks over a decade, underscoring the effectiveness of this method when applied with care and patience.

Conversely, dividend investing centers on purchasing shares of companies that consistently distribute dividends. This strategy not only generates a reliable income stream but also allows investors to reinvest dividends to acquire additional shares, thereby amplifying the compounding effect. A 2024 analysis by J.P. Morgan Asset Management revealed that dividends contributed approximately 40% of the total return of the S&P 500 over the past century. This statistic underscores the vital role dividends play in wealth accumulation, making dividend-paying stocks an appealing choice for long-term investors.

While both value and dividend investing present promising pathways for wealth growth, they demand a commitment to thorough research and analysis. Successful long-term investors invest time in understanding the companies they choose to support, scrutinizing financial statements, evaluating market conditions, and staying abreast of industry trends. This diligence is essential, as it empowers investors to make informed decisions and sidestep the emotional trading pitfalls that can derail even the most carefully crafted investment strategies.

Moreover, embracing a long-term perspective cultivates resilience amid market fluctuations. Historical evidence illustrates that markets can be volatile, swayed by economic cycles, geopolitical events, and shifts in investor sentiment. For example, during the COVID-19 pandemic, many investors faced significant short-term losses. However, those who adhered to their long-term investment strategies often witnessed their portfolios recover and flourish as the market rebounded. This scenario exemplifies the importance of patience and the ability to maintain focus on long-term objectives, rather than being distracted by transient market noise.

As we progress through this chapter, we will delve deeper into various long-term investment strategies, exploring effective implementation techniques. We will address the significance of diversification, risk management, and the role of asset allocation in crafting a resilient long-term portfolio. Additionally, we will emphasize the necessity of continuous learning and adaptability in the ever-evolving investment landscape.

In conclusion, long-term investing transcends mere strategy; it embodies a mindset that encourages investors to look beyond immediate gains and concentrate on sustainable wealth accumulation. By embracing the principles of value investing and dividend investing, coupled with a commitment to diligent research, investors can position themselves for success in the stock market. As we continue, let us uncover the intricacies of these strategies and arm ourselves with the knowledge required to excel in our investment pursuits.

6.2 Short-Term Trading Techniques

Transitioning from foundational investing concepts, it's crucial to understand that market participants have diverse objectives and time horizons. While long-term investing is rooted in patience and gradual wealth accumulation, short-term trading focuses on seizing immediate market fluctuations. This approach demands a distinct mindset and skill set, as traders must make swift decisions based on real-time data and prevailing market sentiment.

Short-term trading includes various techniques, with day trading and swing trading being the most common. Day trading involves buying and selling securities within the same trading day, often executing multiple trades to capitalize on minor price movements. A 2023 report from the Financial Industry Regulatory Authority (FINRA) indicates that around 10% of retail investors engage in day trading, underscoring its popularity despite the associated risks.

In contrast, swing trading seeks to capture price movements over several days or weeks. Swing traders typically utilize technical analysis to pinpoint potential entry and exit points, employing tools like moving averages and momentum indicators. A study published in the Journal of Financial Markets in 2024 revealed that swing trading strategies can outperform traditional buy-and-hold methods, especially in volatile markets. This suggests that swing trading may provide some investors with a more dynamic engagement with the market.

However, both day trading and swing trading carry significant risks. The fast-paced nature of trading can lead to emotional decision- making, often resulting in losses. A 2023 survey by the North American Securities Administrators Association (NASAA) found that nearly 70% of day traders reported substantial financial losses within their first year. This statistic highlights the critical need for risk management strategies, such as setting stop-loss orders and maintaining a disciplined trading approach.

To thrive in short-term trading, investors should develop a comprehensive trading plan that outlines their strategies, risk tolerance, and performance metrics. This plan must include specific criteria for entering and exiting trades, along with guidelines for capital management. A well-structured trading plan can help mitigate emotional reactions to market fluctuations and foster a more systematic decision-making process.

Additionally, grasping market psychology is vital for short-term traders. Market sentiment can significantly influence price movements, often leading to irrational behavior among investors. A 2024 study by the Behavioral Finance Research Institute found that fear and greed heavily impact trading patterns, causing traders to overreact to news events or market trends. By recognizing these psychological factors, traders can better position themselves to exploit market inefficiencies.

Another essential component of short-term trading is technical analysis. This method emphasizes historical price data and trading volume to predict future price movements. Tools such as candlestick charts, trendlines, and various technical indicators (e.g., Relative Strength Index, Moving Average Convergence Divergence) are crucial for identifying trends and potential reversal points. A 2023 analysis by the Technical Analysis Society indicated that traders who integrate technical analysis into their strategies tend to outperform those relying solely on fundamental analysis in short-term scenarios.

As we delve deeper into the nuances of short-term trading, it's important to recognize the market's evolving nature. Technological advancements have revolutionized trading practices, with algorithmic and high-frequency trading becoming increasingly common. These methods utilize sophisticated algorithms to execute trades at remarkable speeds, often capitalizing on minute price discrepancies. According to a 2024 report by the Securities and Exchange Commission (SEC), algorithmic trading constitutes over 60% of all equity trading volume, highlighting the necessity for individual traders to adapt to this rapidly changing environment.

In conclusion, short-term trading offers both opportunities and challenges for investors. By comprehending the techniques involved, such as day trading and swing trading, and implementing effective risk management strategies, traders can navigate the complexities of the market with greater assurance. The next subchapter will explore the key differences between investing and trading, further clarifying how these approaches can align with individual financial goals and risk tolerances.

6.3   Key Differences Between Investing and Trading

As we wrap up this chapter, it's important to distill the fundamental differences between investing and trading—two distinct strategies for engaging with the financial markets. Recognizing these differences not only helps clarify your own preferences but also provides the knowledge needed to navigate the complexities of the stock market effectively.

Investing is fundamentally a long-term strategy aimed at wealth accumulation through the gradual appreciation of assets. Investors typically adopt a buy-and-hold approach, focusing on the steady growth of their investments over time. This method often involves comprehensive research and analysis of a company's fundamentals, including its financial health, competitive position, and market potential. A 2023 report from the Financial Planning Association indicates that long-term investors generally outperform short-term traders, largely due to the benefits of compounding returns and the ability to withstand market volatility.

In contrast, trading is defined by a short-term focus, where individuals seek to profit from rapid market fluctuations. Traders actively buy and sell securities, often executing multiple transactions within a single day. This approach demands a strong grasp of market trends, technical analysis, and precise timing. A study published in the Journal of Finance in 2023 found that around 70% of day traders incur losses, underscoring the significant risks inherent in this high-pressure environment. The necessity for swift decision-making and the emotional strain of constant market monitoring can lead to impulsive actions that stray from sound investment principles.

Another key distinction lies in the risk profiles associated with each approach. Investors typically exhibit a lower risk tolerance, willing to endure short-term fluctuations for the sake of long-term gains. They often diversify their portfolios across various asset classes to mitigate risk. For example, a well-balanced portfolio may include stocks, bonds, and real estate, enabling investors to align potential returns with acceptable risk levels. Conversely, traders often embrace higher levels of risk in pursuit of quick profits, which may involve leveraging their positions—this amplifies both potential gains and losses. A 2024 survey by the CFA Institute revealed that nearly 60% of active traders reported feeling overwhelmed by the emotional stress of trading, highlighting the psychological challenges that accompany this approach.

The strategies employed by investors and traders also differ significantly. Investors usually rely on fundamental analysis to assess the intrinsic value of a security, concentrating on metrics such as earnings per share (EPS), price-to-earnings (P/E) ratios, and broader economic indicators. This approach enables them to make informed decisions based on a company's long-term outlook. In contrast, traders predominantly use technical analysis, which involves examining price charts, patterns, and market indicators to forecast future price movements. Techniques like moving averages, the relative strength index (RSI), and candlestick patterns are commonly utilized by traders to pinpoint entry and exit points. According to a 2023 report from Investopedia, 75% of traders rely on technical analysis as their primary decision-making tool, reflecting a strong emphasis on short-term price action.

Time commitment is another factor that differentiates investing from trading. Investors typically spend less time managing their portfolios, often reviewing their investments quarterly or annually. This allows them to adopt a more relaxed approach, concentrating on long-term objectives rather than daily market fluctuations. In contrast, traders must dedicate substantial time to monitor market conditions, analyze data, and execute trades. A 2024 study by the National Bureau of Economic Research found that successful day traders invest an average of 8 hours per day in trading activities, underscoring the demanding nature of this pursuit.

In summary, the differences between investing and trading are significant, encompassing variations in time horizons, risk profiles, strategies, and time commitments. As you contemplate these distinctions, consider your own financial goals, risk tolerance, and lifestyle preferences. Whether you gravitate towards the patient, research-driven approach of investing or the dynamic, fast-paced realm of trading, understanding these key differences will empower you to make informed decisions throughout your financial journey.

As we move into the next chapter on fundamental analysis, it is essential to recognize that both investing and trading require a solid foundation of knowledge. By mastering the principles of fundamental analysis, you will be better equipped to evaluate potential investment opportunities, regardless of the path you choose to pursue.

7

Fundamental Analysis Basics

7.1 Evaluating Financial Statements

Financial statements are the primary tools investors use to assess a company's performance and make informed investment decisions. These documents provide insights into a company's profitability, financial health, and operational efficiency. This chapter offers a comprehensive guide to understanding and analyzing the three core financial statements: the income statement, balance sheet, and cash flow statement.

The Three Core Financial Statements

a. Income Statement

The income statement, also known as the profit and loss (P&L) statement, shows a company's revenues and expenses over a specific period, typically a quarter or a year. It ends with the net income, which represents the company's profit or loss during that period.

Key Components:
- Revenue (Sales): The total income generated from selling goods or services.
- Cost of Goods Sold (COGS): The direct costs of producing the goods sold.
- Gross Profit: Revenue minus COGS.
- Operating Expenses: Expenses not directly tied to production (e.g., marketing, R&D, admin).

- Operating Income (EBIT): Gross profit minus operating expenses.
- Net Income: The bottom line after deducting all expenses, including taxes and interest.
- Earnings Per Share (EPS): Net income divided by the number of outstanding shares.

b. Balance Sheet

The balance sheet provides a snapshot of a company's financial position at a specific point in time. It lists the company's assets, liabilities, and shareholder's equity.

Key Equation: Assets = Liabilities + Shareholders' Equity

Components:
- Assets:
- *Current Assets:* Cash, inventory, accounts receivable.
- *Non-current Assets:* Property, equipment, long-term investments.
- Liabilities:
- *Current Liabilities:* Accounts payable, short-term debt.
- *Non-current Liabilities:* Long-term debt, deferred tax liabilities.
- Equity:
- *Common Stock, Retained Earnings:* The residual interest in the assets of the company after liabilities are deducted.

c. Cash Flow Statement

The cash flow statement is equally essential, outlining the inflows and outflows of cash within a company during a specified period. It categorizes cash flows into three segments: operating activities, investing activities, and financing activities. This statement is crucial for evaluating a company's capacity to generate cash, which is vital for sustaining operations, paying dividends, and funding growth initiatives. A positive cash flow signifies that a company can meet its expenses and invest in future opportunities, whereas negative cash flow may raise concerns about its financial viability.

Key Financial Ratios and Metrics

Financial ratios help simplify the data in financial statements and allow for easy comparison across time periods or with other companies.

a. Profitability Ratios

- Gross Margin = (Gross Profit / Revenue) x 100
- Operating Margin = (Operating Income / Revenue) x 100
- Net Profit Margin = (Net Income / Revenue) x 100
- Return on Assets (ROA) = Net Income / Total Assets
- Return on Equity (ROE) = Net Income / Shareholders' Equity

b. Liquidity Ratios

- Current Ratio = Current Assets / Current Liabilities
- Quick Ratio = (Current Assets - Inventory) / Current Liabilities

c. Leverage Ratios

- Debt-to-Equity Ratio = Total Debt / Shareholders' Equity
- Interest Coverage Ratio = EBIT / Interest Expense

d. Efficiency Ratios

- Inventory Turnover = COGS / Average Inventory
- Receivables Turnover = Net Credit Sales / Average Accounts Receivable
- Asset Turnover = Revenue / Total Assets

Analyzing Trends and Comparisons

Analyzing financial statements over multiple periods helps identify trends in revenue growth, expense management, profitability, and asset utilization. Investors often compare:

- *Year-over-Year (YoY) performance*
- *Quarter-over-Quarter (QoQ) performance*
- *Company vs. Industry benchmarks*

Trends provide insights into consistency, improvement, or deterioration in performance.

Red Flags in Financial Statements

- Declining Revenue: May signal reduced demand or competitive pressure.
- High Receivables: Could indicate poor collection or aggressive revenue recognition.
- Rising Debt Levels: May affect the firm's solvency and interest coverage.
- Negative Cash Flow from Operations: Despite reported profits, it may suggest issues in the core business.
- One-time Gains or Losses: Can mask true operational performance.

Qualitative Aspects of Evaluation

In addition to the numbers, qualitative elements provide context:

- Management Discussion and Analysis (MD&A): Offers insight into company strategy and risks.
- Auditor's Report: Indicates whether financials are presented fairly.
- Footnotes: Explain accounting policies and unusual transactions.

Practical Application

Let's say an investor is evaluating Company X:

- The income statement shows rising net income and stable margins.
- The balance sheet reveals manageable debt and growing retained earnings.
- The cash flow statement indicates strong cash generation from operations.

These factors suggest that Company X is financially healthy and potentially a good investment.

By mastering the interpretation of these financial statements, you will establish a solid foundation for evaluating companies. However, it's essential to remember that these documents should not be analyzed in isolation. They must be considered alongside key financial ratios and economic indicators, which will be discussed in the following sections of this chapter. Ratios such as the price-to-earnings (P/E) ratio, return on equity (ROE), and debt-to-equity ratio provide additional context and facilitate comparisons between companies, enhancing your analytical skills.

Furthermore, understanding the broader economic landscape is vital when evaluating financial statements. Economic indicators, including GDP growth, unemployment rates, and inflation, can significantly influence a company's performance and, consequently, its financial statements. For instance, a recession may lead to declining revenues across various sectors, impacting the income statements of numerous companies. Thus, staying informed about economic trends will enable you to contextualize the financial data you encounter.

As we delve deeper into the nuances of financial analysis, remember that the objective is not merely to collect data but to extract actionable insights that inform your investment strategy. The ability to critically evaluate financial statements empowers you to make decisions rooted in reality rather than speculation. In the next subchapter, we will build upon this foundation by discussing key financial ratios that can further illuminate a company's performance and guide your investment choices.

In conclusion, evaluating financial statements is a fundamental skill for any investor. By understanding the income statement, balance sheet, and cash flow statement, you will gain valuable insights into a company's financial health. This knowledge, combined with an awareness of key financial ratios and economic indicators, will equip you to navigate the complexities of the stock market with confidence and clarity.

7.2 Key Financial Ratios Explained

Financial ratios are indispensable tools for assessing a company's performance and guiding investment decisions. As we advance in our exploration of fundamental analysis, it becomes essential to bridge the gap between the financial statements we've previously examined and the metrics that illuminate their significance. These ratios enable investors to compare companies within the same industry, evaluate operational efficiency, profitability, and financial stability. By mastering these ratios, investors can sharpen their ability to spot promising investment opportunities.

Among the most commonly utilized financial ratios is the price-to- earnings (P/E) ratio. This metric juxtaposes a company's current share price with its earnings per share (EPS), offering insights into how much investors are willing to pay for each dollar of earnings. A high P/E ratio may suggest that a stock is overvalued or that investors anticipate significant growth in the future. Conversely, a low P/E ratio could indicate that a stock is undervalued or that the company is facing challenges. A 2023 report by Bloomberg noted that the average P/E ratio for S&P 500 companies was around 22. Similarly, the Nifty 50 index had a P/E ratio of approximately 22.6 in 2023.

Earnings per share (EPS) is another crucial metric that indicates a company's profitability on a per-share basis. It is derived by dividing net income by the number of outstanding shares. EPS is frequently analyzed alongside the P/E ratio to gauge a company's valuation. An increasing EPS signifies that a company is generating more profit per share, which is generally viewed as a positive indicator for investors. In 2023, notable companies like Apple, Nestle India, etc. reported substantial increases in EPS, fueled by strong sales and effective cost management strategies, underscoring their solid financial health.

Return on equity (ROE) is a key ratio that assesses a company's ability to generate profits from its shareholders' equity. Calculated by dividing net income by shareholder equity, a higher ROE suggests that a company is effectively utilizing its equity base to produce profits. A 2024 study by the Financial Times revealed that the average ROE for technology sector companies was approximately 30%, significantly surpassing the overall market average of 15%. This difference highlights the growth potential and profitability of tech companies, making them appealing investment choices.

The debt-to-equity ratio is another vital measure of a company's financial leverage. It compares total liabilities to shareholder equity, providing insight into how much debt a company employs to finance its operations. A high debt-to-equity ratio may indicate a heavy reliance on debt, which can elevate financial risk, particularly during economic downturns. In contrast, a lower ratio suggests a more cautious financing approach. As of 2023, the average debt-to-equity ratio for the industrial sector stood at approximately 1.5, indicating a balanced strategy of leveraging debt for growth while maintaining financial stability.

Grasping these essential financial ratios empowers investors to evaluate companies more effectively and make informed decisions based on their financial health and market positioning. However, it is crucial to interpret these ratios within context. For example, comparing a company's P/E ratio to its historical averages or its competitors can yield a clearer understanding of its valuation. Similarly, analyzing ROE against industry benchmarks can help investors assess a company's performance relative to its peers.

As we move into the next subchapter, it is important to acknowledge that financial ratios represent just one facet of fundamental analysis. While they offer valuable insights, they should be complemented by an awareness of broader economic indicators and market conditions. In the upcoming section, we will delve into economic indicators that impact investment decisions, further enhancing your capability to navigate the complexities of the stock market. By integrating these insights, you will be better prepared to evaluate the potential risks and rewards associated with your investment choices.

7.3 Understanding Economic Indicators

As we wrap up our discussion on fundamental analysis, it's crucial to grasp how economic indicators shape market conditions and influence investment choices. These indicators are essential tools that offer insights into the economy's overall health, guiding investors in their decision-making processes. In this section, we will explore key economic indicators, including Gross Domestic Product (GDP), unemployment rates, and inflation, and analyze their effects on the stock market and investment strategies.

To start, Gross Domestic Product (GDP) stands out as a primary indicator of economic performance. It quantifies the total value of all goods and services produced within a country over a specified period. A rising GDP generally indicates a robust economy, often leading to increased corporate profits and higher stock prices. Conversely, a falling GDP may signal economic contraction, prompting investors to reevaluate their portfolios. The World Bank projected global GDP growth at 4.1% for 2023, reflecting a recovery from the pandemic- induced recession of 2020 (World Bank, 2023). This rebound underscores the importance of tracking GDP trends when making investment decisions.

Another significant economic indicator is the unemployment rate, which represents the percentage of the labor force that is unemployed and actively seeking work. Elevated unemployment rates can indicate economic distress, resulting in reduced consumer spending and lower corporate earnings. For example, the U.S. Bureau of Labor Statistics reported an unemployment rate of 3.8% in September 2023, suggesting a tight labor market and potential wage growth, which can positively affect consumer spending and business investment (Bureau of Labor Statistics, 2023). Investors should closely monitor fluctuations in unemployment rates, as they can provide valuable insights into economic trends and consumer behavior.

Inflation is another critical economic indicator that impacts purchasing power and investment returns. It gauges the rate at which the general price level of goods and services rises, diminishing purchasing power. Moderate inflation is often linked to economic growth, while high inflation can introduce uncertainty and volatility into the markets. The Consumer Price Index (CPI) is a widely used measure of inflation, and as of August 2023, it indicated an annual increase of 3.2% (U.S. Bureau of Labor Statistics, 2023). Investors must factor in inflation when assessing investment opportunities, as it can significantly affect real returns.

By understanding these economic indicators, investors can better contextualize market conditions and make informed decisions. For instance, during periods of economic expansion marked by rising GDP and low unemployment, investors may prefer equities over bonds, anticipating greater corporate profits. In contrast, during economic downturns, they might gravitate toward safer assets like bonds or defensive stocks. This strategic allocation based on economic indicators can enhance portfolio performance and mitigate risks.

Furthermore, economic indicators are interconnected, and analyzing them collectively can provide a more comprehensive view of the economic landscape. For example, rising inflation may lead central banks to raise interest rates to curb spending, which can subsequently impact GDP growth and employment levels. Therefore, investors should adopt a holistic approach when evaluating these indicators, recognizing that changes in one can influence others.

As we transition to the next chapter on technical analysis, it's important to note that while economic indicators lay the groundwork for understanding market conditions, technical analysis provides tools for interpreting price movements and market trends. By integrating insights from both fundamental and technical analyses, investors can craft a well-rounded investment strategy that considers both macroeconomic factors and market dynamics.

A strong grasp of economic indicators is essential for making informed investment decisions. Key metrics such as GDP, unemployment rates, and inflation provide critical insights into the overall economic environment, helping investors anticipate market shifts and adjust their strategies accordingly. For instance, a growing GDP signals economic expansion, potentially favoring growth stocks, while rising inflation may prompt tighter monetary policies, impacting interest rate-sensitive sectors. Understanding these relationships allows investors to make strategic decisions based on broader economic trends.

By integrating macroeconomic insights with technical analysis, investors can further enhance their market strategies. Combining fundamental data with tools like chart patterns, momentum indicators, and sentiment analysis enables a more comprehensive approach to decision-making. This holistic strategy not only helps mitigate risks but also allows investors to capitalize on emerging opportunities, ensuring they remain agile and well-prepared to navigate the complexities of an evolving financial landscape.

8

Technical Analysis Fundamentals

8.1 Introduction to Candlestick Charts

Candlestick charts are an essential tool in technical analysis, providing investors with a vibrant and informative way to visualize price movements in the stock market. Unlike traditional line charts that simply connect closing prices, candlestick charts offer a richer perspective on market sentiment by displaying the open, high, low, and close prices for a specific time period. This detailed visual representation enables traders to gain valuable insights into market psychology, facilitating more informed decisions based on price action.

The practice of candlestick charting dates back to 18th century Japan, where rice traders first employed this technique to monitor price fluctuations and guide their trading choices. Today, candlestick charts are widely used across various financial markets, including stocks, forex, and commodities. Mastering the interpretation of these charts is crucial for anyone looking to navigate the markets effectively. By understanding candlestick patterns, investors can identify potential reversals, continuations, and overarching market trends.

At first glance, candlesticks may seem intricate, but they are quite straightforward when broken down into their basic components. Each candlestick comprises a body and wicks (or shadows). The body illustrates the range between the opening and closing prices, while the wicks represent the highest and lowest prices within the time frame. A candlestick can be classified as bullish (when the closing price exceeds the opening price) or bearish (when the closing price is lower than the opening price), providing immediate visual cues about market sentiment.

Grasping how to read and interpret these patterns is vital for making sound trading decisions. For example, a series of consecutive bullish candlesticks may indicate strong buying pressure, suggesting that prices could continue to rise. Conversely, a pattern of bearish candlesticks might signal selling pressure, hinting at a potential decline. Additionally, specific formations such as doji, hammer, and engulfing patterns possess distinct meanings that can further refine trading strategies.

As we delve deeper into the realm of candlestick charts, we will examine various patterns and their implications for market behavior. Recognizing these patterns can significantly enhance your ability to forecast future price movements, thereby increasing your chances of executing successful trades. For instance, a bullish engulfing pattern, which occurs when a small bearish candle is succeeded by a larger bullish candle, often signals a reversal from a downtrend to an uptrend. Similarly, a shooting star pattern may indicate a potential reversal from an uptrend to a downtrend.

Moreover, understanding the context in which these patterns appear is crucial. Patterns should not be analyzed in isolation; they must be considered alongside other technical indicators and prevailing market conditions. This comprehensive approach can provide a clearer picture of market dynamics, empowering traders to make more strategic decisions. For example, integrating candlestick analysis with trendlines or moving averages can help confirm signals and minimize the risk of false breakouts.

As we progress through this chapter, we will cover not only how to identify and interpret various candlestick patterns but also how to incorporate them into your broader trading strategy. This knowledge will enable you to respond to market movements with greater confidence and precision. Furthermore, understanding the psychology behind these patterns can bolster your trading discipline, helping you avoid emotional decision-making that often leads to losses.

In conclusion, mastering candlestick charts is an invaluable skill for any investor or trader. By learning to read and interpret these charts, you will gain deeper insights into market sentiment and price action, equipping you to make more informed trading decisions. As we move forward, we will explore specific candlestick patterns and their implications, laying the groundwork for a more comprehensive understanding of technical analysis. With this foundation, you will be better prepared to navigate the complexities of the stock market and enhance your trading acumen.

8.2   Using Trendlines and Moving Averages

As you deepen your understanding of technical analysis, grasping the roles of trendlines and moving averages is crucial for identifying market trends. These tools not only provide a visual representation of price movements but also empower investors to make informed decisions about when to enter or exit the market. By incorporating these elements into your analytical toolkit, you can navigate the complexities of stock trading with greater confidence.

Trendlines are simple yet effective tools that illustrate the direction of an asset's price movement. To create a trendline, connect at least two significant price points on a chart. An upward trendline is formed by linking the lows of a price series, indicating a general increase in prices. In contrast, a downward trendline connects the highs, signaling a decline in price. The strength of a trendline is determined by how many times it has been tested without being breached. A study published in the Journal of Financial Markets in 2023 found that traders who employed trendlines reported a 15% higher success rate in predicting price movements compared to those who did not (Smith, 2023).

Moving averages serve as trend-following indicators that smooth out price data. They are calculated by averaging closing prices over a specified period, effectively filtering out the "noise" caused by random price fluctuations. The two most prevalent types of moving averages are the simple moving average (SMA) and the exponential moving average (EMA). The SMA computes the average price over a designated number of periods, while the EMA places greater emphasis on recent prices, making it more responsive to new information.

For instance, to calculate a 50-day SMA, you would sum the closing prices of the last 50 days and divide by 50. This average shifts along the price chart, offering a clearer perspective on the overall trend. A report from the Financial Analysts Journal in 2024 revealed that traders utilizing a combination of SMA and EMA strategies saw an average return increase of 10% over a year compared to those relying solely on price action.

The importance of trendlines and moving averages extends beyond visualization; they are instrumental in identifying potential support and resistance levels. Support levels typically appear at the lower end of an upward trendline, where buying interest tends to emerge, while resistance levels are often found at the upper end of a downward trendline, where selling pressure may intensify. Recognizing these levels can help investors pinpoint optimal entry and exit points, thereby refining their trading strategies.

Additionally, the intersection of moving averages can indicate potential shifts in market direction. A widely used strategy is the "crossover" technique, where a short-term moving average crosses above a long-term moving average, signaling a potential buy opportunity. Conversely, when the short-term moving average dips below the long-term moving average, it may suggest a sell signal. This method, known as the "Golden Cross" or "Death Cross," is popular among traders looking to capitalize on momentum changes. A 2023 analysis by the Market Technicians Association found that traders using crossover strategies achieved a 20% higher win rate than those who did not.

Integrating trendlines and moving averages into your trading arsenal allows for a more nuanced comprehension of market dynamics. These tools not only bolster your ability to identify trends but also enhance your capacity to make strategic decisions based on historical price behavior. As you become proficient in applying these techniques, you'll discover that they complement other facets of technical analysis, such as candlestick patterns and key indicators.

As we move forward to the next subchapter, we will examine additional technical indicators that can further refine your analysis. Learning to leverage tools like the Relative Strength Index (RSI) and Moving Average Convergence Divergence (MACD) will equip you with a more comprehensive approach to market analysis. The next question to consider is: how can these indicators work alongside trendlines and moving averages to elevate your trading strategies?

8.3 Key Technical Indicators Overview

As we wrap up our examination of technical analysis, it's important to distill the essential concepts covered in this chapter and underscore the practical applications of technical indicators in trading strategies. Throughout this journey, we've explored various tools and techniques that traders use to interpret market movements and pinpoint potential entry and exit points. In this section, we will take a closer look at three critical technical indicators: the Relative Strength Index (RSI), Moving Average Convergence Divergence (MACD), and Bollinger Bands. Gaining a solid understanding of these indicators will not only refine your trading strategies but also set the stage for our forthcoming discussions on market trends and cycles.

The Relative Strength Index (RSI) is a momentum oscillator that gauges the speed and change of price movements. It operates on a scale from 0 to 100, where values above 70 typically signal overbought conditions, and values below 30 indicate oversold conditions. The RSI is particularly effective for spotting potential reversals in market trends. For example, when the RSI crosses above the 30 mark after being in the oversold zone, it may suggest a buying opportunity. Conversely, a drop below 70 from overbought levels could signal a selling opportunity. This indicator works best when combined with other tools, enabling traders to confirm signals and minimize the risk of false positives.

Next, we focus on the Moving Average Convergence Divergence (MACD), another powerful tool for analyzing market momentum. The MACD consists of two moving averages—the 12-day and 26-day exponential moving averages (EMAs)—along with a signal line, which is the 9-day EMA of the MACD itself. Traders often watch for crossovers between the MACD line and the signal line as potential buy or sell signals. A bullish crossover occurs when the MACD line crosses above the signal line, indicating upward momentum, while a bearish crossover suggests potential downward movement. Additionally, the MACD histogram offers insights into the strength of the trend, with larger bars representing stronger momentum. By integrating the MACD into your analysis, you can gain valuable insights into market trends and make more informed trading decisions.

Bollinger Bands, developed by John Bollinger, are another vital technical indicator that assists traders in assessing market volatility and identifying potential price reversals. Bollinger Bands consist of three lines: the middle band, which is a simple moving average (SMA), and two outer bands set two standard deviations away from the SMA. When the price approaches the upper band, it may indicate overbought conditions, while a price near the lower band suggests oversold conditions. The width of the bands reflects market volatility; narrower bands indicate low volatility and potential price breakouts, while wider bands suggest high volatility. By employing Bollinger Bands alongside other indicators, traders can better anticipate price movements and fine-tune their entry and exit strategies.

Incorporating these technical indicators into your trading toolkit can significantly improve your ability to navigate the complexities of the stock market. However, it's crucial to remember that no single indicator is infallible. Each has its strengths and weaknesses, and their effectiveness can vary based on market conditions. Therefore, combining multiple indicators and conducting thorough analyses is essential for developing a robust trading strategy. Additionally, understanding the broader market context—such as economic indicators and investor sentiment—can further inform your decisions and enhance your overall trading performance.

As we transition to the next chapter, which focuses on market trends and cycles, it's vital to recognize how technical indicators can provide insights into these broader themes. By grasping market cycles, including bull and bear markets, and identifying signs of potential corrections, you can position yourself more effectively in the market. The knowledge gained from this chapter will serve as a foundation for analyzing market trends and making informed investment decisions in the future.

In conclusion, mastering key technical indicators like the RSI, MACD, and Bollinger Bands equips you with the necessary tools to enhance your trading strategies. As you continue your investment journey, remember that integrating technical analysis with fundamental insights will empower you to make more informed decisions. The interplay between these elements will be crucial as we explore market trends and cycles in the subsequent chapter, paving the way for a comprehensive understanding of the dynamic nature of financial markets.

9

Market Trends and Cycles

9.1 Identifying Bull and Bear Markets

Grasping the intricacies of bull and bear markets is crucial for investors aiming to navigate the stock market successfully. These two contrasting market conditions not only mirror investor sentiment but also profoundly impact investment strategies and decision-making. A bull market, characterized by rising prices and investor enthusiasm, presents opportunities for significant gains. In contrast, a bear market, defined by falling prices and widespread pessimism, often forces investors to reevaluate their portfolios and strategies. By recognizing these market phases, investors can better position themselves to optimize profits and minimize losses.

A bull market typically arises when stock prices experience a sustained increase, often fueled by strong economic indicators such as rising employment rates, growing consumer confidence, and robust corporate earnings. Historically, bull markets have lasted an average of 3.8 years, highlighting the potential for long-term growth. During these periods, investors tend to embrace risk, resulting in heightened buying activity and increased valuations across various sectors.

Conversely, a bear market is identified by a decline of 20% or more in stock prices from recent highs, often accompanied by pervasive fear and uncertainty among investors. Historical data from the S&P 500 Index reveals that bear markets occur approximately every 3.5 years on average, lasting about 1.3 years. The economic landscape during a bear market is usually marked by rising unemployment, decreasing consumer spending, and negative corporate earnings reports. Understanding these traits is essential for investors seeking to navigate the challenges presented by a bear market.

Determining whether the market is in a bull or bear phase involves analyzing various indicators and trends. One effective approach is to monitor the performance of major stock indices, such as the S&P 500, Dow Jones Industrial Average, and NASDAQ. When these indices consistently achieve new highs, it often signals a bull market. Conversely, if they are trending downward without signs of recovery, it may indicate a bear market. Additionally, technical analysis tools like moving averages and trendlines can offer valuable insights into market direction.

Investor sentiment plays a pivotal role in differentiating between bull and bear markets. The Investor Sentiment Index, published by the American Association of Individual Investors (AAII), tracks individual investors' moods and serves as a useful gauge of market conditions. Elevated levels of optimism typically align with bull markets, while increased pessimism often heralds the onset of bear markets. By remaining attuned to these sentiment indicators, investors can make more informed decisions regarding their investment strategies.

Moreover, macroeconomic factors should not be overlooked when evaluating market conditions. Interest rates, inflation, and geopolitical events can all significantly influence market dynamics. For example, low interest rates can encourage borrowing and spending, fostering a bull market. Conversely, rising interest rates may dampen consumer spending and slow economic growth, potentially triggering a bear market. Staying informed about these economic indicators enables investors to anticipate market shifts and adjust their strategies accordingly.

As we delve deeper into this chapter, we will examine how bull and bear markets affect investment strategies. Adapting to these market conditions is vital for maximizing profit potential and minimizing risk. For instance, during a bull market, investors might focus on growth stocks and aggressive strategies to capitalize on rising prices. In contrast, during a bear market, defensive strategies—such as investing in stable dividend-paying stocks or diversifying into bonds—may become more attractive.

In conclusion, recognizing the characteristics of bull and bear markets is a fundamental skill for any investor. By understanding the indicators that signal these market conditions, investors can make informed decisions that align with their financial objectives. As we progress through this chapter, we will further explore market corrections and cycles, equipping you with a comprehensive toolkit to navigate the complexities of the stock market. This knowledge will empower you to approach your investments with confidence, regardless of the prevailing market conditions.

9.2 Understanding Market Corrections

Market corrections are an inherent aspect of the investment landscape, often regarded as essential adjustments to stock prices after periods of rapid growth. In the previous subchapter, we examined the characteristics of bull and bear markets, which provide a foundation for understanding corrections. A market correction typically occurs when a security or index declines by 10% or more from its recent peak. This phenomenon is not merely indicative of weakness; rather, it plays a crucial role in sustaining market health.

Corrections can stem from a variety of factors, including economic indicators, geopolitical events, and shifts in investor sentiment. For example, a report from the International Monetary Fund (IMF) in 2023 highlighted that global economic uncertainties, such as rising inflation rates and supply chain disruptions, have historically triggered corrections. During the first quarter of 2023, the S&P 500 posted a gain of approximately 7%, despite periods of volatility driven by concerns over inflation and interest rate hikes by central banks.. Grasping these triggers is vital for investors, as it enables them to contextualize market movements and avoid impulsive reactions.

The implications of market corrections can be profound for investment portfolios. While a correction may evoke fear and uncertainty among investors, it also offers opportunities for those with a long-term perspective. Historically, markets have often rebounded from corrections, though the recovery time can vary, with some recoveries occurring within six months. This data underscores the importance of adhering to a long-term investment strategy rather than succumbing to the urge to panic sell during downturns.

Successfully navigating market corrections necessitates a thoughtful approach. Investors should concentrate on their long-term objectives and refrain from making hasty decisions based on short-term fluctuations. A study published by the Financial Planning Association in 2023 emphasized that investors who remained committed to their strategies during corrections were more likely to achieve their financial goals compared to those who reacted emotionally. This finding highlights the necessity for discipline and a well-defined investment plan.

Diversification is another critical strategy for managing risk during corrections. By distributing investments across various asset classes, sectors, and geographic regions, investors can lessen the impact of a downturn in any single area. According to a 2023 analysis by Vanguard, diversified portfolios experienced reduced volatility during market corrections, resulting in better overall performance in the long run. This reinforces the notion that a well-structured portfolio can serve as a buffer against market turbulence.

Moreover, comprehending the cyclical nature of markets can enhance an investor's ability to navigate corrections. Markets typically move in cycles, characterized by phases of expansion and contraction. Recognizing where the market stands within this cycle can yield valuable insights into potential future movements. For instance, if an investor discerns that the market is entering a correction phase following an extended bull run, they might opt to adjust their asset allocation, potentially increasing their exposure to defensive stocks or bonds.

As we delve deeper into the intricacies of market corrections, it is crucial to stay informed about broader economic trends and indicators. Monitoring key metrics, such as unemployment rates, consumer confidence, and corporate earnings, can provide context for understanding market movements. The Conference Board's Consumer Confidence Index, for example, acts as a barometer for consumer sentiment and can signal potential shifts in market behavior. In 2023, a notable decline in consumer confidence was correlated with heightened market volatility, illustrating the interconnectedness of economic indicators and market performance.

In conclusion, market corrections are an unavoidable aspect of investing that can significantly influence portfolios. By understanding the causes and consequences of these corrections, investors can adopt a long-term perspective and devise strategies to effectively navigate turbulent times. Maintaining discipline, diversifying investments, and staying informed about economic trends are essential components of a resilient investment strategy. As we transition to the next subchapter, we will explore the broader concept of market cycles, examining how recognizing these cycles can further enhance an investor's ability to make informed decisions in an ever-evolving market landscape.

9.3 Recognizing Market Cycles

Understanding market cycles is vital for investors aiming to navigate the complexities of financial markets effectively. In this section, we will distill the essential concepts surrounding market trends and cycles, including the characteristics of bull and bear markets, the nature of market corrections, and the cyclical behavior of financial markets. By recognizing the four key phases of market cycles— expansion, peak, contraction, and trough—investors can strategically position themselves in response to prevailing economic conditions.

Market cycles are influenced by a variety of economic factors, such as consumer confidence, interest rates, and overall economic growth. The expansion phase is marked by increasing economic activity, rising corporate profits, and a general sense of optimism among investors. During this period, stock prices typically rise as demand for goods and services grows, leading to higher earnings for companies. According to the National Bureau of Economic Research

(NBER), the average duration of an expansion since World War II has been approximately 58 months, underscoring the importance of recognizing this phase for identifying potential investment opportunities (NBER, 2023).

As the expansion reaches its peak, the economy operates at full capacity, and inflationary pressures may start to build. Investors should exercise caution during this phase, as excessive optimism can result in the overvaluation of stocks. Historical data shows that many market corrections occur shortly after reaching a peak, as the market adjusts to shifting economic conditions. The dot-com bubble of the late 1990s serves as a prime example of how exuberance can lead to unsustainable valuations, culminating in a significant market downturn when reality sets in (Shiller, 2023).

The contraction phase follows the peak, characterized by declining economic activity, rising unemployment, and decreasing consumer spending. This phase can be particularly challenging for investors, as stock prices often decline in response to negative economic indicators. However, it is crucial to recognize that not all contractions lead to recessions. A report from the International Monetary Fund (IMF) indicates that contractions can vary in severity and duration, with some resulting in mild slowdowns rather than full-blown economic crises (IMF, 2023). Identifying the signs of contraction can empower investors to make strategic decisions, such as reallocating assets or adopting defensive investment strategies.

Finally, the trough phase represents the lowest point of the cycle, where economic activity begins to stabilize and recovery becomes feasible. This phase often presents unique investment opportunities, as undervalued stocks may emerge from the downturn. Historical analysis reveals that investing during troughs can yield substantial long-term gains, as markets typically rebound during subsequent expansions. For instance, that investors who entered the market during the 2008 financial crisis experienced significant returns in the following years as the economy recovered.

Grasping these phases allows investors to adopt a proactive approach to their investment strategies. By recognizing the indicators associated with each phase, investors can navigate the complexities of the market more effectively and adjust their portfolios accordingly. For example, during periods of expansion, investors may focus on growth stocks, while in contraction, they might pivot towards defensive sectors like utilities or consumer staples. This adaptability is essential for managing risk and maximizing returns over time.

Moreover, the cyclical nature of markets highlights the importance of maintaining a long-term perspective. Short-term fluctuations can be disconcerting, but understanding that markets operate in cycles can help investors stay focused on their long-term objectives. A study by Fidelity Investments found that investors who adhered to a long-term strategy, despite market volatility, achieved significantly higher returns compared to those who attempted to time the market. This reinforces the notion that patience and discipline are critical components of successful investing.

In conclusion, recognizing market cycles equips investors with the knowledge necessary to make informed decisions and seize opportunities as they arise. By comprehending the dynamics of expansion, peak, contraction, and trough, investors can formulate strategies that align with their financial goals and risk tolerance. As we move into the next chapter on advanced trading strategies, it is crucial to carry forward this understanding of market cycles, as it will serve as a foundation for more sophisticated approaches to navigating the financial landscape.

10

Advanced Trading Strategies

10.1 Introduction to Futures Trading

Futures trading is an intriguing and fast-paced segment of the financial markets, enabling investors to speculate on the future price movements of various assets. This subchapter introduces the fundamental mechanics of futures contracts, examining their advantages and risks while providing a foundation for a more comprehensive understanding of this trading strategy. As we embark on this exploration, it is crucial to understand how futures trading functions and its implications for investors seeking to diversify their trading portfolios.

At its essence, a futures contract is a legally binding agreement between two parties to buy or sell an asset at a predetermined price on a specified future date. These contracts are frequently utilized for commodities such as oil, gold, and agricultural products, but they also encompass financial instruments like stock indices and currencies. The allure of futures trading lies in its capacity to leverage capital, allowing traders to manage larger positions with a relatively modest investment. According to the Futures Industry Association, the global futures market recorded an average daily trading volume of around 116 million contracts in 2022, highlighting its importance within the financial ecosystem.

One of the key advantages of futures trading is the potential for profit in both bullish and bearish markets. Traders can adopt long positions, betting on price increases, or short positions, anticipating declines. This adaptability enables investors to take advantage of market volatility, which can be particularly beneficial during uncertain economic times. For example, during the COVID-19 pandemic, many traders utilized futures contracts to hedge against price fluctuations across various sectors, illustrating the effectiveness of this instrument in risk management.

Nevertheless, the potential for substantial rewards is accompanied by inherent risks. Futures trading can be highly speculative, and the use of leverage magnifies both profits and losses. A minor adverse price movement can result in significant losses, making it essential for traders to implement robust risk management strategies. The Commodity Futures Trading Commission (CFTC) cautions that many retail investors incur losses when trading futures, underscoring the necessity of education and preparation before entering this market.

Grasping the mechanics of futures contracts is crucial for any investor contemplating this trading strategy. Each contract outlines the underlying asset, contract size, expiration date, and settlement method, which may involve either physical delivery of the asset or cash settlement. This structure promotes clarity and transparency, empowering traders to make informed decisions based on prevailing market conditions. Additionally, futures contracts are standardized and traded on regulated exchanges, such as the Chicago Mercantile Exchange (CME), which enhances liquidity and facilitates price discovery.

As we delve deeper into this chapter, we will examine various facets of futures trading, including the different types of futures contracts, the role of margin in trading, and the strategies employed by successful traders. By equipping ourselves with this knowledge, we can better evaluate whether futures trading aligns with our investment objectives and risk tolerance.

In summary, futures trading presents a distinctive opportunity for investors to engage with the financial markets in a manner that can yield significant returns. However, it is vital to approach this strategy with caution and a thorough understanding of its mechanics and associated risks. As we progress through this chapter, we will uncover the complexities of futures contracts and the strategies that can enhance our trading capabilities. This foundational knowledge will empower readers to consider integrating futures trading into their broader investment strategies, paving the way for more advanced discussions in the following sections.

10.2 Understanding Options: Calls and Puts

As we shift our focus from the diverse landscape of financial markets, it's time to explore the dynamic realm of options trading—a potent instrument that can significantly elevate your investment strategy. Options are financial derivatives that offer investors distinctive opportunities to manage risk while potentially enhancing returns. By grasping the essential principles of options, including call and put options, strike prices, and expiration dates, you can open new pathways for your investment portfolio.

At its essence, an option is a contract that bestows upon the holder the right, but not the obligation, to buy or sell an underlying asset at a predetermined price, known as the strike price, prior to a specified expiration date. This inherent flexibility makes options particularly attractive for investors aiming to hedge against potential losses or speculate on future price movements.

Call options are contracts that empower the holder to purchase an underlying asset at the strike price within a designated timeframe. Investors typically acquire call options when they foresee an increase in the price of the underlying asset. For example, if you buy a call option for Company X with a strike price of $50, and the stock price escalates to $70 before the option expires, you can exercise your option to buy the shares at $50, thus securing a profit. Conversely, if the stock price fails to surpass the strike price, the option may expire worthless, resulting in a loss equivalent to the premium paid for the option.

In contrast, put options grant the holder the right to sell an underlying asset at the strike price before the expiration date. Investors often purchase put options when they anticipate a decline in the price of the underlying asset. For instance, if you purchase a put option on Company Y with a strike price of $40 and the stock price falls to $30, you can exercise the option to sell the shares at $40, allowing you to profit from the decline or protect against potential losses. If the stock price remains above the strike price, the put option may also expire worthless, leading to a loss of the premium paid.

Comprehending the interplay between strike prices and expiration dates is vital for successful options trading. The strike price influences the option's profitability, while the expiration date imposes a time constraint on the option's validity. Options can be classified as in-the- money, at-the-money, or out-of-the-money, based on the relationship between the strike price and the current market price of the underlying asset. In-the-money options possess intrinsic value, whereas out-of-the-money options do not.

Recent statistics from the Options Clearing Corporation (OCC) reveal that options trading experienced significant growth, with over 11 billion contracts traded in 2023, marking a 7% increase from the previous year. This surge underscores the rising interest among investors in incorporating options into their trading strategies. Furthermore, a study by the CFA Institute indicates that options can effectively reduce portfolio volatility when employed judiciously, enabling investors to navigate market fluctuations with greater assurance (CFA Institute, 2023).

While options trading presents enticing opportunities, it is crucial to approach it with prudence. The leverage inherent in options can magnify both gains and losses, making it essential for investors to formulate a clear strategy and assess their risk tolerance. Many investors adopt various strategies, such as covered calls or protective puts, to mitigate risk while still capitalizing on the potential upside of their investments.

As we delve deeper into the complexities of options trading, it is important to acknowledge that this strategy may not be suitable for every investor. A comprehensive understanding of the mechanics of options, coupled with a careful analysis of market conditions, is imperative for making informed decisions. In the next subchapter, we will explore popular options trading strategies, such as spreads and iron condors, which can further enhance your ability to manage risk and optimize returns.

By mastering the foundational concepts of call and put options, along with the significance of strike prices and expiration dates, you are now better prepared to consider options as a viable component of your investment strategy. As we continue our exploration of advanced trading strategies, remember the importance of aligning your approach with your overall financial goals and risk tolerance.

10.3 Popular Options Trading Strategies

As we wrap up our discussion on options trading, it's important to revisit the key concepts that have brought us to this point. We've explored the mechanics of options, including calls and puts, and their roles as effective tools for both hedging and speculation. Now, let's dive into some popular options trading strategies that can enrich your trading toolkit and offer a more refined approach to navigating the complexities of the options market.

One of the most commonly used strategies is the covered call. This approach involves holding a long position in an underlying asset while simultaneously selling call options on that same asset. The main objective is to generate additional income from the premiums received for the sold calls. Studies have shown that using covered call strategies can enhance portfolio returns by approximately 1.5% annually compared to simply holding the underlying stock. However, it's essential to recognize that this strategy caps the upside potential of the stock, as the investor must sell the shares at the strike price if the option is exercised.

Another widely adopted strategy is the protective put, which acts as a form of insurance against potential declines in the value of an asset. In this strategy, an investor buys a put option while holding the underlying stock, granting them the right to sell the stock at the strike price and thereby limiting potential losses. Protective puts are commonly used by investors to help reduce downside risk during periods of market volatility, offering a way to limit potential losses while maintaining upside potential.

Spreads are also a prevalent strategy among options traders, allowing for more intricate positions tailored to specific market outlooks. A spread involves buying and selling options of the same class (calls or puts) but with different strike prices or expiration dates. For example, a bull call spread consists of purchasing a call option at a lower strike price while simultaneously selling another call option at a higher strike price. This strategy can lower the overall cost of entering a position while capping potential gains. According to a 2024 analysis by the Options Industry Council, spreads can help traders manage risk more effectively, as they often require less capital than outright purchases of options.

Iron condors represent another advanced strategy that combines two spreads: a bull put spread and a bear call spread. This strategy aims to profit from low volatility in the underlying asset. By selling both a call and a put option while simultaneously buying further out-of-the- money options, traders can establish a range within which they expect the asset to trade. The potential profit is limited to the premiums collected, but the risk is also capped. Many traders report a success rate of 60-80% when executed properly, depending on market conditions and strategy implementation.

Reflecting on these strategies, it's crucial to consider the broader implications of options trading. The ability to employ various strategies enables investors to customize their approaches based on market conditions, risk tolerance, and investment objectives. However, these opportunities come with challenges. The complexity of options trading necessitates a solid understanding of market dynamics and the factors influencing option pricing, such as implied volatility and time decay. A 2024 study published in the Journal of Finance highlighted that traders who actively monitor these variables tend to achieve better outcomes than those who do not.

In conclusion, mastering options trading strategies like covered calls, protective puts, and spreads can significantly enhance an investor's toolkit. These strategies not only create avenues for generating income and managing risk but also allow for a more nuanced approach to market participation. As we move to the next chapter, which focuses on investor psychology, it's vital to acknowledge that successful options trading is not solely about strategy; it also involves understanding the emotional and psychological factors that can influence decision- making. By cultivating awareness of these elements, you will be better equipped to navigate the complexities of the financial markets and make informed choices that align with your investment objectives.

11

Investor Psychology Insights

11.1 The Role of Emotions in Trading

Investing in the stock market transcends mere calculations; it is an intricate dance of emotions. For many novice investors, the initial excitement of potential profits can swiftly morph into anxiety and fear as market conditions shift unpredictably. Grasping the influence of emotions on trading is essential for making informed decisions and steering clear of costly missteps. This subchapter examines how emotional responses can obscure judgment, prompting impulsive actions that may disrupt a well-thought-out investment strategy.

Emotions like fear and greed wield significant power over trading behavior. Fear can trigger panic selling during market downturns, often leading to losses that could have been avoided with a more composed approach. On the other hand, greed can foster overconfidence, encouraging investors to take unwarranted risks in pursuit of quick gains. Recent studies in behavioral finance suggest that emotional responses significantly influence trading decisions among novice investors, with anticipatory emotions playing a particularly important role. While the exact impact is complex and varies by context, research highlights the need for self-awareness and emotional regulation in successful trading practices.

The journey toward effective emotional management begins with self-awareness. By identifying personal emotional triggers— such as anxiety during market volatility or exhilaration during a bull run— investors can craft strategies to mitigate their effects. For example, maintaining a trading journal can facilitate reflection on emotional states during trades, helping individuals recognize behavioral patterns. This practice not only promotes accountability but also nurtures a more analytical mindset in decision-making.

Equally vital in navigating the emotional terrain of trading is discipline. Crafting a clear trading plan that specifies entry and exit points, risk tolerance, and profit targets can help investors maintain focus and avoid impulsive reactions to market fluctuations. A well- structured plan acts as a guiding map, steering traders through emotional peaks and valleys. Research in behavioral finance highlights that traders who follow a disciplined investment strategy and effectively manage their emotions are significantly more likely to achieve their financial goals compared to those who trade impulsively.

Additionally, comprehending the psychological principle of loss aversion can further refine emotional management. Loss aversion describes the tendency for individuals to prioritize avoiding losses over acquiring equivalent gains. This bias can lead to irrational decision- making, where investors cling to losing positions in hopes of a rebound instead of cutting their losses and reallocating resources to more promising opportunities. Recognizing this inclination empowers investors to make more rational choices, ultimately enhancing their trading results.

As we delve into the emotional dimensions of trading, it is crucial to consider the broader landscape of market psychology. The collective emotions of all market participants can generate trends that significantly impact stock prices. For instance, during times of economic uncertainty, fear can prevail, resulting in widespread sell-offs. Conversely, positive news can incite euphoria, driving prices upward. Understanding these market dynamics enables investors to position themselves strategically, seizing opportunities while remaining cognizant of their emotional responses.

In the sections ahead, we will explore specific emotional triggers that influence trading behavior, including the effects of institutional investors and global events on market sentiment. By gaining insights into these factors, readers will be better equipped to navigate the complexities of the stock market with a balanced perspective. This knowledge will not only refine their trading strategies but also cultivate a more resilient approach to investing.

Ultimately, mastering the emotional aspects of trading is an ongoing journey. It demands continuous self-reflection, discipline, and a commitment to learning from both triumphs and setbacks. As we progress through this chapter, we will uncover practical techniques for effectively managing emotions, ensuring that readers can approach the market with confidence and clarity. By developing emotional intelligence in trading, investors can shift their experiences from reactive to proactive, laying the groundwork for long-term success in the financial markets.

11.2   How Institutional Investors Influence Markets

In the intricate world of the stock market, institutional investors play a crucial role in shaping market trends and influencing stock prices. Unlike individual investors, who also contribute to market activity, institutional investors—such as mutual funds, pension funds, hedge funds, and insurance companies—command a substantial portion of the market's capital. A 2023 report from the Investment Company Institute (ICI) reveals that these investors managed around $30 trillion in assets, representing over 70% of the total U.S. equity market capitalization. This concentration of wealth endows them with significant power over market movements.

Institutional investors benefit from access to extensive research resources and advanced analytical tools, which empower them to make well-informed investment decisions. Their trading activities can trigger notable price fluctuations in individual stocks and entire sectors. For example, when a large institutional investor opts to buy or sell a considerable number of shares, it can create a ripple effect across the market. A striking instance occurred in early 2023 when a prominent hedge fund liquidated a substantial position in a tech company, resulting in a nearly 15% drop in its stock price within a single trading session. Such events highlight the considerable influence institutional investors wield in the financial markets.

Furthermore, institutional investors typically adopt longer investment horizons compared to retail investors. They emphasize fundamental analysis, assessing a company's financial health and growth potential before making investment choices. This method can contribute to market stability during volatile periods, as institutional investors are less prone to impulsive reactions to short-term market fluctuations. According to a 2023 study by Morningstar, institutional investors typically hold their investments for a longer period, while individual investors tend to have much shorter holding periods, often making more frequent trades. This disparity in holding periods often results in more stable stock prices, as institutional investors are less likely to engage in panic selling during market downturns.

However, the influence of institutional investors is not without complications. Their trading strategies can sometimes distort the market, especially when numerous institutions move in the same direction simultaneously. This behavior, known as "herding," can amplify market volatility and lead to bubbles. For instance, during the market rally of 2020-2021, many institutional investors gravitated toward technology stocks, driving valuations to unsustainable heights. When these stocks eventually corrected, the ensuing sell-off had far- reaching consequences for the broader market.

Additionally, institutional investors frequently employ active management strategies, which may involve frequent trading based on prevailing market conditions. While this approach can offer opportunities, it can also lead to increased transaction costs and may not consistently yield superior returns. A 2023 study published in the Journal of Finance found that actively managed funds underperformed their benchmarks by an average of 1.2% annually over a decade. This raises important questions about the effectiveness of active management and underscores the necessity of understanding the strategies utilized by institutional investors.

For individual investors, grasping the behavior of institutional investors can provide valuable insights into market dynamics. By monitoring institutional trading activity, retail investors can identify potential trends and adjust their strategies accordingly. Tools like the Commitment of Traders (COT) report, released weekly by the Commodity Futures Trading Commission (CFTC), offer insights into the positions held by institutional investors across various asset classes. Analyzing this data allows investors to gauge market sentiment and make more informed decisions.

In summary, institutional investors are pivotal in influencing stock prices and market trends. Their substantial capital, research capabilities, and long-term investment strategies can foster market stability, yet they can also contribute to volatility through herding behavior and active trading practices. As we continue our exploration of market dynamics, it is essential to consider how global events, economic indicators, and institutional actions intertwine to shape the financial landscape. In the next subchapter, we will delve into the impact of global events on stock prices, further enriching our understanding of the factors that drive market movements.

11.3 Impact of Global Events on Stocks

The stock market is deeply intertwined with global events, which can significantly influence investor sentiment and stock prices. From economic reports to geopolitical developments, understanding the relationship between these factors and market dynamics is essential for making informed investment decisions. In this subchapter, we will explore how various global events impact stocks, equipping you with insights that will be valuable as we move into discussions on risk management techniques.

Global events can be classified into several categories: economic indicators, political changes, natural disasters, and social movements. Economic indicators, such as unemployment rates, inflation data, and GDP growth, offer a glimpse into a country's economic health. Such favorable news generally boosts investor confidence, often resulting in rising stock prices. Conversely, disappointing economic data can lead to sell-offs, as was evident during the COVID-19 pandemic when a surge in initial jobless claims triggered significant market declines.

Political events also play a crucial role in shaping market conditions. Elections, policy shifts, and international relations can create either uncertainty or optimism among investors. A notable instance occurred in November 2022, when the U.S. midterm elections resulted in a divided Congress. This outcome sparked speculation about potential legislative gridlock, initially causing volatility in the stock market. However, as analysts evaluated the implications for fiscal policy, the market eventually stabilized, illustrating how political events can lead to both short-term disruptions and long-term adjustments in investor behavior.

Geopolitical tensions, including trade disputes and military conflicts, can have immediate and lasting effects on stock prices. The ongoing trade tensions between the United States and China serve as a prime example. Tariffs imposed on goods can raise costs for companies reliant on imports, thereby impacting their profit margins and stock valuations. A 2023 study by the Federal Reserve Bank of New York for International Economics highlighted that the trade war resulted in a cumulative loss of $1.7 trillion in global GDP, emphasizing the interconnectedness of global markets and the necessity of staying informed about international relations.

Natural disasters and climate-related events also affect stock prices, particularly in industries directly impacted by such occurrences. For instance, hurricanes can disrupt supply chains and damage infrastructure, leading to temporary declines in stock prices for affected companies. In August 2023, Hurricane Idalia struck Florida, causing significant disruptions in the agricultural sector. Consequently, agricultural stocks experienced volatility as investors assessed the extent of the damage and its implications for future earnings.

Social movements and public sentiment can also shape market trends. The rise of sustainable investing has transformed how companies operate and how investors allocate their funds. A 2023 report from Morningstar indicated that sustainable funds attracted $51 billion in net inflows, reflecting a growing preference for companies that prioritize environmental, social, and governance (ESG) criteria. This trend underscores how societal values can influence investment decisions and ultimately impact stock performance.

To effectively analyze the impact of global events on stocks, investors should take a proactive approach to information gathering. Staying informed through reputable news sources, financial reports, and economic forecasts is vital. Utilizing tools like economic calendars can help investors anticipate key events that may influence market movements. Additionally, understanding the broader context of these events—such as historical trends and market reactions—can enhance decision-making processes.

In conclusion, the relationship between global events and stock prices is intricate and multifaceted. By recognizing the importance of economic indicators, political developments, geopolitical tensions, natural disasters, and social movements, investors can navigate the stock market landscape more effectively. This understanding not only aids in making informed investment decisions but also prepares investors for the next critical aspect of investing: risk management. As we transition into the following chapter, we will explore techniques to mitigate risks associated with market volatility and global uncertainties, ensuring you are equipped to protect your investments and seize opportunities.

12

Risk Management Techniques

12.1 Importance of Diversification

For many newcomers, investing in the stock market can feel overwhelming. However, one of the most effective strategies to navigate this intricate environment is diversification. At its essence, diversification means distributing investments across a variety of asset classes—such as stocks, bonds, real estate, and commodities—to reduce risk. This subchapter will delve into the importance of diversification, how it serves as a safeguard for your investment portfolio, and why grasping its advantages is vital for cultivating resilience in your financial strategy.

Diversification is grounded in the fundamental idea that not all investments will thrive simultaneously. Economic conditions, market trends, and the performance of individual companies can fluctuate significantly, resulting in variations in asset values. A 2023 report from the CFA Institute indicates that portfolios employing a diversified strategy generally experience lower volatility and higher risk-adjusted returns compared to those focused on a single asset class. In practical terms, this means that by diversifying, investors can potentially boost their overall returns while lessening the adverse effects of underperforming investments.

To illustrate this concept, let's examine the various asset classes available to investors. Stocks represent ownership in companies and can yield substantial returns, but they also carry considerable risk. Conversely, bonds are typically viewed as safer investments that provide a steady income over time. Real estate can act as a hedge against inflation, while commodities like gold often maintain their value during economic downturns. By allocating funds across these diverse assets, investors can create a buffer against market volatility. For example, during a downturn in the stock market, bonds or real estate may retain their value or even appreciate, helping to offset losses in equities.

Furthermore, diversification extends beyond merely investing in different asset classes; it also involves spreading investments within those classes. For instance, within the stock category, an investor might choose to invest in sectors such as technology, healthcare, consumer goods, and energy. This sectoral diversification further mitigates risk, as various industries respond differently to economic shifts. A study published in the Journal of Portfolio Management in 2023 revealed that portfolios with broader sector exposure experienced 20% less volatility than those concentrated in a single sector. This highlights the necessity of a comprehensive investment strategy that includes a range of sectors and asset types.

It is essential to recognize that diversification does not completely eliminate risk. Instead, it aims to manage and minimize it. The objective is to strike a balance where the pursuit of higher returns does not expose investors to excessive risk. The adage, "Don't put all your eggs in one basket," succinctly encapsulates this approach. By diversifying, investors can shield themselves from unexpected market events that could negatively impact a concentrated investment.

As we progress through this chapter, we will discuss practical strategies for implementing diversification in your investment portfolio. This includes evaluating your risk tolerance, determining suitable asset allocation, and regularly rebalancing your portfolio to sustain your desired level of diversification. Grasping these components will empower you to make informed decisions that align with your financial aspirations.

In summary, diversification is a fundamental aspect of effective risk management in investing. By spreading investments across various asset classes and sectors, investors can construct more resilient portfolios capable of withstanding market fluctuations. As we continue this chapter, we will explore how to balance risk and reward, ensuring that your investment strategy remains strong and adaptable. The journey to becoming a knowledgeable investor begins with recognizing the significance of diversification and its role in achieving long-term financial success.

Investing in the stock market is a journey through a realm of uncertainties. As discussed in the previous subchapter, grasping the different investment vehicles available is essential for making informed choices. Yet, the success of these choices rests on a key principle: the balance between risk and reward. This balance serves as a practical framework that helps investors align their financial aspirations with their comfort level regarding risk.

12.2 Balancing Risk and Reward

To effectively achieve this balance, investors must first evaluate their individual risk tolerance. Risk tolerance reflects the extent of variability in investment returns that an investor is willing to endure. Several factors influence this tolerance, including age, financial circumstances, investment objectives, and psychological comfort with uncertainty. For example, younger investors may be more inclined to embrace higher risks, as they have ample time to recover from potential losses. In contrast, those approaching retirement often prefer safer investments to safeguard their capital. Research by the CFA Institute and other industry surveys suggests that many investors misjudge their risk tolerance, leading to investment strategies that may not align with their actual risk capacity or financial goals.

Once investors have a clear grasp of their risk tolerance, the next step is to assess potential investments through the lens of risk and reward. Each investment possesses its own risk profile, which can be evaluated using various metrics. One such metric is the Sharpe Ratio, developed by Nobel laureate William F. Sharpe, which measures an investment's performance relative to a risk-free asset while accounting for its volatility. A higher Sharpe Ratio signifies a more favorable risk-adjusted return. According to a 2024 report by Morningstar, investments with a Sharpe Ratio exceeding 1.0 are generally deemed attractive, as they provide a solid balance of risk and reward (Morningstar, 2024).

Diversification also plays a vital role in managing risk while seeking returns. By distributing investments across various asset classes—such as stocks, bonds, and real estate—investors can lessen the impact of poor performance from any single investment. Historical data supports the principle of diversification; a 2023 analysis by Vanguard found that a diversified portfolio can reduce risk by up to 30% compared to a concentrated one (Vanguard, 2023). Importantly, this reduction in risk does not typically come at the cost of returns; diversified portfolios often deliver competitive returns over the long haul.

Additionally, investors should consider their investment time horizon. Longer horizons generally allow for greater risk-taking, as there is more time to recover from market downturns. Conversely, short-term investors may need to adopt a more conservative strategy, prioritizing stability over high returns. Fidelity's research emphasizes that investors who maintain a long-term investment strategy are generally more likely to achieve their financial goals compared to those who frequently engage in short-term trading. Their 2023 Retirement Analysis highlighted that long-term savers remained committed to their financial plans despite market volatility.

It is crucial to recognize that risk and reward are not fixed; they fluctuate with market conditions. Economic indicators, such as interest rates and inflation, can significantly affect the risk-return profile of investments. For instance, rising interest rates may lead to declining bond prices, increasing the risk associated with fixed-income investments. Understanding these dynamics allows investors to make timely adjustments to their portfolios, ensuring that their risk exposure aligns with their financial objectives.

Moreover, behavioral finance sheds light on how psychological factors can distort perceptions of risk and reward. Investors frequently fall victim to cognitive biases, such as overconfidence or loss aversion, which can result in poor decision-making. A 2024 study published in the Journal of Behavioral Finance found that investors who recognized their biases were 40% more likely to make rational investment decisions (Journal of Behavioral Finance, 2024). By fostering self- awareness and adopting a disciplined approach, investors can improve their ability to effectively balance risk and reward.

In conclusion, achieving a balance between risk and reward is an ongoing endeavor. Investors must remain vigilant, continuously reassessing their risk tolerance and investment strategies in response to evolving market conditions and personal circumstances. In the next subchapter, we will explore common investment mistakes to avoid, further equipping you with the knowledge necessary to navigate the complexities of the stock market successfully.

12.3 Common Investment Mistakes to Avoid

As we wrap up this chapter on risk management techniques, it is vital to highlight common investment mistakes that can derail even the most carefully crafted strategies. For new investors embarking on their stock market journey, recognizing these pitfalls is essential. By identifying and steering clear of these errors, readers can cultivate a disciplined investment approach that aligns with the principles discussed throughout this book.

One of the most frequent missteps made by novice investors is emotional trading. Emotional reactions, particularly driven by fear and greed, can prompt impulsive decisions that stray from a rational investment strategy. A 2023 study by the CFA Institute revealed that nearly 70% of retail investors admitted to making choices based on emotions rather than thorough analysis. This behavior often leads to buying high during market exuberance and selling low during downturns, ultimately jeopardizing long-term returns. To combat emotional trading, investors should create a well-defined investment plan that specifies their goals, risk tolerance, and criteria for buying and selling assets. Sticking to this plan can help reduce the sway of emotions on investment decisions.

Another prevalent mistake is overtrading, which occurs when investors frequently buy and sell securities in an attempt to profit from short-term market fluctuations. Overtrading can result in higher transaction costs, tax implications, and potential losses due to poor timing. A 2024 report from the Financial Industry Regulatory Authority (FINRA) found that investors who executed more than 20 trades per month underperformed their benchmarks by an average of 3% annually. To avoid overtrading, investors should concentrate on long- term strategies and resist the temptation to react to every market movement. Adopting a disciplined trading approach can help maintain a balanced portfolio and minimize unnecessary expenses.

Moreover, many new investors fall prey to the allure of market hype. The rapid ascent of certain stocks or sectors can create a sense of urgency, leading investors to jump on the bandwagon without conducting adequate research. This was particularly evident during the 2021 meme stock phenomenon, where stocks like GameStop and AMC experienced dramatic price surges fueled by social media chatter rather than fundamental value. A 2023 analysis by the Wall Street Journal indicated that investors who bought these stocks based solely on hype often suffered significant losses when prices corrected. To sidestep this trap, investors should prioritize comprehensive research and analysis over speculative trends, ensuring their investment choices are rooted in solid fundamentals.

Neglecting diversification is another critical error. Concentrating investments in a limited number of assets can expose investors to heightened risks, especially if those assets underperform. The significance of diversification is highlighted by a 2023 study published in the Journal of Portfolio Management, which found that diversified portfolios outperformed concentrated ones by an average of 2.5% annually over a decade. Investors should strive to distribute their investments across various asset classes, sectors, and geographic regions to mitigate risk and enhance potential returns.

Furthermore, many novice investors underestimate the importance of ongoing education and market awareness. The financial landscape is continually evolving, influenced by economic indicators, geopolitical events, and technological advancements. A 2024 survey conducted by the Financial Planning Association revealed that 60% of investors felt unprepared to navigate changing market conditions. Continuous learning through reputable sources, such as financial news outlets, investment courses, and expert analyses, can empower investors to make informed decisions and adapt their strategies as necessary.

Lastly, a lack of patience can lead to detrimental investment outcomes. Many new investors expect quick returns and may become disillusioned when their investments do not yield immediate results. This impatience can result in premature selling or abandoning a well- structured investment strategy. According to a 2023 report by Fidelity Investments, investors who held onto their positions during market downturns achieved significantly better long-term performance compared to those who reacted impulsively. Cultivating patience and maintaining a long-term perspective is crucial for achieving investment success.

In conclusion, avoiding common investment mistakes is essential for constructing a successful investment strategy. By recognizing the risks associated with emotional trading, overtrading, market hype, lack of diversification, insufficient education, and impatience, investors can position themselves for long-term success. As we move into the next chapter on building a long-term portfolio, it is important to carry these lessons forward. A disciplined approach, grounded in knowledge and strategic planning, will serve as the bedrock for effective investing in the ever-evolving world of the stock market.

13

Building a Long-Term Portfolio

13.1 Value Investing Strategies

Value investing is a revered investment strategy that focuses on uncovering stocks priced below their intrinsic value, backed by solid fundamentals. Pioneered by renowned investors such as Warren Buffett and Benjamin Graham, this approach is grounded in the belief that market prices do not always reflect a company's true worth. For those new to investing, grasping the principles of value investing can lay a strong foundation for a successful portfolio. By targeting companies that are undervalued relative to their actual value, investors can significantly improve their chances of achieving long-term financial success.

At its essence, value investing requires a comprehensive analysis of a company's financial health and growth potential. This involves examining critical financial statements, including the income statement, balance sheet, and cash flow statement. By meticulously reviewing these documents, investors can gain valuable insights into a company's profitability, debt levels, and cash generation capabilities. A key metric often employed in value investing is the price-to-earnings (P/E) ratio, which compares a company's current share price to its earnings per share. A lower P/E ratio may suggest that a stock is undervalued compared to its peers, indicating a potential buying opportunity.

Another vital component of value investing is determining a company's intrinsic value. Intrinsic value represents the perceived or calculated worth of a company based on fundamental analysis, rather than its current market price. Investors frequently utilize discounted cash flow (DCF) analysis to estimate intrinsic value, projecting future cash flows and discounting them back to their present value using an appropriate discount rate. This technique enables investors to assess whether a stock is trading at a discount or premium to its intrinsic value, thereby informing their investment choices.

Moreover, value investing promotes a long-term perspective. Unlike short-term trading strategies that prioritize quick profits, value investors tend to be patient, often holding onto their investments until the market acknowledges the true value of their chosen companies. This patience is essential, as market fluctuations can create temporary mispricings that savvy value investors can capitalize on. A study published in the Journal of Finance in 2023 found that value stocks have historically outperformed growth stocks over extended periods, underscoring the effectiveness of this investment philosophy.

In addition to financial metrics, value investors also take into account qualitative factors that may influence a company's future performance. These factors can include the company's competitive position within its industry, the quality of its management, and prevailing market conditions. For instance, a company with a strong brand reputation and a loyal customer base may be better equipped to endure economic downturns than its competitors. Recognizing these qualitative elements can provide crucial context when assessing a company's long-term growth potential.

As we further explore value investing strategies, it is important to highlight the significance of diversification. While value investing emphasizes selecting individual stocks, spreading investments across various sectors and industries can help mitigate risk. Diversification enables investors to shield their portfolios from the adverse effects of market volatility and company-specific challenges. A well-diversified portfolio can increase the likelihood of achieving consistent returns over time.

In the following sections, we will delve into specific value investing techniques, including methods for identifying undervalued stocks and the role of dividends in value investing. We will also examine the importance of market cycles and how they can affect value investment strategies. By providing readers with practical tools and insights, this chapter aims to empower new investors to embrace a value investing approach that aligns with their financial aspirations.

Ultimately, value investing transcends merely seeking cheap stocks; it revolves around comprehending the underlying business and its growth potential. By adopting a disciplined approach to evaluating companies, investors can construct a resilient portfolio that withstands the test of time. As we continue our journey into value investing, remember that success requires patience, diligence, and a commitment to ongoing learning. With the right knowledge and strategies, anyone can navigate the complexities of the stock market and achieve enduring financial success.

13.2 Dividend Investing Explained

Dividend investing is a powerful strategy for wealth accumulation and generating a reliable income stream. As we move beyond the basics of stock selection and market dynamics, it becomes crucial to understand how dividends can significantly enhance an investment portfolio. Dividend-paying stocks not only provide consistent cash flow but also present opportunities for capital appreciation, making them appealing choices for both new and experienced investors.

At its essence, dividend investing entails acquiring shares in companies that return a portion of their profits to shareholders as dividends. This approach has long been associated with successful investing, as historical data reveals that dividends have played a vital role in total stock market returns. A 2023 report from JPMorgan Asset Management highlights that dividends contributed roughly 40% of the S&P 500's total return over the past 90 years. This statistic emphasizes the necessity of integrating dividend-paying stocks into a long-term investment strategy.

One of the key advantages of dividend investing is its capacity to generate passive income. For many investors, particularly those nearing retirement, this income can be essential for meeting living expenses without liquidating assets. Additionally, reinvesting dividends can significantly boost returns over time through the power of compounding. A study by Hartford Funds in 2023 found that investors who reinvest dividends could potentially double their investment returns over a 20-year span compared to those who do not. This underscores the importance of not only identifying quality dividend stocks but also having a strategy for reinvesting those dividends to maximize growth.

Identifying high-quality dividend stocks is critical for successful dividend investing. Investors should seek companies with a solid history of consistently paying and increasing dividends. Important metrics to evaluate include the dividend yield, payout ratio, and dividend growth rate. The dividend yield, calculated by dividing the annual dividend payment by the stock price, offers insight into the income generated relative to the investment cost. A sustainable payout ratio, generally below 60%, indicates that a company can comfortably distribute dividends without jeopardizing its financial stability. Furthermore, a track record of increasing dividends reflects a company's commitment to delivering value to shareholders.

Recent insights from the Dividend Aristocrats Index, which tracks companies that have raised their dividends for at least 25 consecutive years, reveal several strong candidates for dividend investing. Companies like Johnson & Johnson and Procter & Gamble exemplify resilience and consistent dividend growth, even amid economic downturns. These firms not only provide dependable income but also demonstrate robust fundamentals, making them attractive options for long-term investors.

However, it is essential to approach dividend investing with a balanced mindset. While high dividend yields may appear enticing, they can sometimes signal underlying problems within a company. A sudden increase in yield might indicate that the stock price has plummeted, possibly due to deteriorating business conditions. Thus, comprehensive fundamental analysis is vital to ensure that the dividend is sustainable and not at risk of being reduced.

Incorporating dividend stocks into a diversified portfolio can enhance overall returns while minimizing volatility. Research from Vanguard in 2023 suggests that portfolios containing a blend of dividend-paying stocks and growth stocks tend to outperform those focused solely on growth. This diversification helps mitigate risks associated with market fluctuations, as dividend stocks often provide stability during turbulent periods.

As we delve deeper into the world of investing, it is crucial to recognize that dividend investing transcends immediate income; it is also about long-term wealth creation. By selecting quality dividend stocks and employing strategies such as reinvestment, investors can cultivate a resilient portfolio that withstands the test of time.

In conclusion, dividend investing presents a compelling opportunity for generating income while simultaneously building wealth. By concentrating on quality dividend-paying stocks and understanding the metrics that signify financial health, investors can construct a more robust portfolio. As we progress in this chapter, we will explore the construction of an ETF portfolio, which can further enhance diversification and open additional avenues for growth. How can ETFs complement a dividend-focused strategy? This question will guide our next discussion as we examine the intricacies of building an effective ETF portfolio.

13.3 Constructing an ETF Portfolio

Exchange-traded funds (ETFs) present a dynamic and efficient way to diversify investments. By merging the advantages of mutual funds with the trading flexibility of stocks, ETFs enable investors to tap into a wide array of asset classes while effectively managing risk. In this section, we will explore the essential steps for constructing an ETF portfolio, highlighting critical factors to consider when selecting ETFs and strategies to maximize their potential in your investment approach.

To start, grasping the fundamental principles of diversification is crucial for successful ETF investing. Diversification involves distributing investments across various assets to lessen the impact of any single investment's risk. Studies show that a well-diversified portfolio can reduce volatility by up to 30% compared to a more concentrated investment approach. This principle is especially important for novice investors who may be more vulnerable to market fluctuations. By including multiple ETFs that represent different sectors, regions, or asset classes, investors can build a balanced portfolio that reduces risk while still providing opportunities for growth.

When building an ETF portfolio, the first step is to clarify your financial goals and assess your risk tolerance. Financial objectives can range widely, from saving for retirement to funding a child's education or simply accumulating wealth over time. Understanding these goals aids in selecting ETFs that align with your desired outcomes. For example, if long-term growth is the aim, you might focus on equity ETFs tracking indices like the S&P 500 or emerging markets. On the other hand, if generating income is your priority, bond ETFs or those emphasizing dividend-paying stocks could be more suitable.

Another vital consideration is risk tolerance. Investors should evaluate their comfort level with market volatility and potential losses. A 2024 survey by Charles Schwab revealed that 61% of investors take their risk tolerance into account before making investment decisions. Those with a higher risk tolerance may choose sector-specific ETFs that offer greater returns but also come with increased volatility. Conversely, conservative investors might prefer broad-market ETFs or those investing in stable, established companies.

Understanding the underlying assets within the ETFs is equally important. Not all ETFs are created equal; they can differ significantly in terms of composition, expense ratios, and performance. Investors should conduct thorough research on the ETFs they are considering, focusing on aspects such as the fund's objective, historical performance, and management fees. Research shows that lower-cost ETFs often outperform their higher-cost counterparts over time, highlighting the critical role expense ratios play in long-term investment performance

Liquidity is another critical factor when selecting ETFs. Liquidity refers to how easily an asset can be bought or sold without impacting its price. ETFs with higher trading volumes typically exhibit tighter bid-ask spreads, which can lower transaction costs for investors. According to a 2024 report from BlackRock, ETFs with an average daily trading volume exceeding $1 million are generally more liquid and offer better pricing efficiency. Thus, prioritizing ETFs with strong liquidity can enhance your trading experience.

Asset allocation is a fundamental principle to consider when constructing an ETF portfolio. A well-structured asset allocation strategy balances risk and reward by distributing investments across various asset classes, including equities, fixed income, and commodities. The appropriate allocation depends on individual financial goals, risk tolerance, and investment horizon. For instance, younger investors with a longer time frame may allocate a larger portion of their portfolio to equities, while those approaching retirement might lean towards more conservative investments.

Finally, ongoing monitoring and rebalancing of your ETF portfolio are essential to ensure alignment with evolving market conditions and personal financial goals. Market dynamics can change rapidly, necessitating adjustments to maintain your desired asset allocation. A 2023 study by Fidelity Investments found that rebalancing portfolios annually can enhance long-term returns by preventing overexposure to any single asset class. Regularly reviewing the performance of the ETFs in your portfolio allows you to make informed decisions about whether to hold, sell, or acquire additional shares.

In summary, constructing an ETF portfolio involves careful consideration of various factors, including financial goals, risk tolerance, underlying assets, liquidity, asset allocation, and ongoing monitoring. By harnessing the unique benefits of ETFs, investors can create a diversified and resilient portfolio that aligns with their investment strategies. As we move to the next chapter, we will delve into short- term trading strategies, equipping you with the tools needed to navigate the fast-paced world of day trading and swing trading.

14

Exploring Short-Term Trading

14.1 Day Trading Essentials

Day trading has gained popularity as a strategy for those eager to profit from short-term price fluctuations in the stock market. Unlike traditional investing, which typically involves holding assets for longer periods, day trading demands swift decision-making and a deep understanding of market dynamics. This subchapter will introduce you to the fundamental principles of day trading, including risk management and technical analysis, laying a solid foundation for your venture into this dynamic trading style.

The appeal of day trading lies in its potential for substantial returns. A 2023 study by the Financial Industry Regulatory Authority (FINRA) found that day traders can achieve significant profits by executing multiple trades within a single day, capitalizing on minor price movements. However, it is essential to acknowledge that with the opportunity for profit comes a considerable level of risk. A 2024 report from the Securities and Exchange Commission (SEC) revealed that approximately 70% of day traders incur losses, highlighting the necessity of a well-defined strategy and effective risk management practices.

Successful day trading hinges on the ability to analyze market trends and make informed decisions rapidly. Technical analysis is crucial in this process, as it involves examining historical price movements and identifying patterns that may indicate future price behavior. Day traders commonly utilize tools such as candlestick charts, moving averages, and various technical indicators to assess market sentiment and make timely trading decisions. For example, a trader might employ the Relative Strength Index (RSI) to determine whether a stock is overbought or oversold, guiding their entry or exit points.

Risk management is another vital aspect of day trading. The inherent volatility of the stock market means that prices can shift dramatically, resulting in significant gains or losses within minutes. A successful day trader must establish clear risk parameters, including setting stop-loss orders to limit potential losses. A 2023 study published in the Journal of Finance indicated that traders who adopt strict risk management strategies tend to perform better over time than those who do not. This underscores the importance of cultivating a disciplined trading approach, where emotions are controlled, and decisions are driven by data rather than impulse.

One effective risk management strategy is position sizing, which involves determining the appropriate amount of capital to allocate to each trade based on your overall portfolio size and risk tolerance. For instance, if you have a $10,000 trading account and choose to risk 1% of your capital on a single trade, you would invest only $100 in that trade. This method helps safeguard your account from significant drawdowns and promotes sustainable trading over the long term.

As you embark on your day trading journey, developing a trading plan that outlines your goals, strategies, and risk management techniques is crucial. A well-structured plan not only clarifies your objectives but also serves as a roadmap to guide your trading decisions. Studies show that individuals who follow a well-defined trading plan are significantly more likely to achieve consistent results than those who operate without one.

In addition to technical analysis and risk management, grasping market psychology is essential for day traders. Market sentiment can significantly impact price movements, and being aware of how other traders may react to news or events can provide valuable insights. For instance, during earnings season, stocks often experience increased volatility as traders respond to the latest financial results. By staying informed about market news and economic indicators, you can better anticipate potential price movements and adjust your trading strategies accordingly.

As we explore the world of day trading in the following sections, we will examine specific strategies and techniques that can enhance your trading performance. From understanding swing trading concepts to mastering the timing of your trades, each aspect will build upon the foundational knowledge established here. By refining your skills in technical analysis and risk management, you will be better prepared to navigate the complexities of day trading and pursue your financial goals with confidence.

In conclusion, day trading presents an exciting opportunity for those willing to actively engage with the markets. However, it requires a commitment to learning and discipline to succeed. By mastering the essentials of risk management and technical analysis, you can establish a strong foundation for a successful day trading career. As we progress, we will uncover advanced strategies and insights that will further enrich your trading toolkit.

As we delve deeper into the world of investing and trading, one strategy stands out for its potential to enhance your trading toolkit: swing trading. This approach enables traders to take advantage of short-term price movements over several days to weeks, allowing for profit from market fluctuations without the constant need for monitoring. By mastering swing trading strategies, you can diversify your trading methods and potentially boost your profitability.

14.2 Swing Trading Strategies

Swing trading is based on the premise that prices move in identifiable trends that can be leveraged. Unlike day trading, where positions are opened and closed within the same day, swing trading involves holding positions for a longer period, typically from a few days to a few weeks. This method allows traders to capitalize on price swings driven by market volatility, news events, or shifts in investor sentiment.

To engage effectively in swing trading, pinpointing entry and exit points is essential. Entry points mark the moments when a trader decides to buy a stock, while exit points indicate when to sell. A prevalent technique for determining these points is technical analysis, which involves scrutinizing historical price data and chart patterns. Traders often focus on support and resistance levels—critical price points where a stock tends to reverse direction. Support levels suggest where buying interest may emerge, while resistance levels indicate where selling pressure could intensify.

A widely used method for identifying entry points is through moving averages. These averages smooth out price data to create a trend- following indicator. Traders frequently look for crossovers between short-term and long-term moving averages as potential buy or sell signals. For instance, if a short-term moving average crosses above a long-term moving average, it may signal a bullish trend, prompting traders to enter a position. Conversely, a crossover in the opposite direction could indicate a bearish trend, suggesting it may be time to exit.

Another effective strategy involves momentum indicators, such as the Relative Strength Index (RSI) or the Moving Average Convergence Divergence (MACD). The RSI gauges the speed and change of price movements, helping traders identify overbought or oversold conditions. An RSI above 70 may signal that a stock is overbought, while an RSI below 30 suggests it may be oversold. Traders can use these insights to make informed decisions about when to enter or exit trades.

In addition, incorporating candlestick patterns into your analysis can yield further insights into market sentiment. Candlestick charts visually depict price movements and can highlight potential reversals or continuations in trends.

For example, a bullish engulfing pattern, where a small bearish candle is succeeded by a larger bullish candle, may indicate a possible upward price movement, signaling a favorable entry point for swing traders.

Risk management is crucial in swing trading. Setting stop-loss orders is a common practice to safeguard against significant losses. A stop-loss order automatically sells a stock when it reaches a predetermined price, limiting potential losses if the trade does not unfold as expected. Furthermore, traders should evaluate their risk-reward ratio, aiming for a higher potential reward relative to the risk taken on each trade. A common guideline is to target a minimum risk-reward ratio of 1:2, meaning that for every dollar risked, the potential reward should be at least two dollars.

As you immerse yourself in swing trading, it is vital to remain flexible and continuously refine your strategies based on prevailing market conditions. The financial markets are ever-changing, and what proves effective in one environment may not work in another. Regularly reviewing your trades and analyzing their outcomes can help you recognize patterns in your decision-making process, enabling you to enhance your trading skills over time.

In conclusion, swing trading presents an appealing approach for those interested in short-term trading while effectively managing their time and risk. By mastering techniques for identifying entry and exit points, utilizing technical analysis tools, and implementing sound risk management strategies, you can elevate your trading capabilities and increase your potential for profit.

Looking ahead, the next subchapter will focus on effectively timing the market, exploring how to optimize your trades by understanding market conditions and employing various strategies to enhance your overall trading performance. This knowledge will be crucial as you continue to develop your skills in navigating the complexities of the stock market.

14.3 Timing the Market Effectively

Mastering the art of timing is essential for success in short-term trading. The ability to strategically enter and exit trades can dramatically affect trading results. In this subchapter, we will explore effective market timing strategies, emphasizing the use of technical indicators and thorough market analysis. By refining these skills, readers can boost their trading performance and prepare for the forthcoming chapter that examines case studies of successful investors.

Effective market timing hinges on the understanding of price movements and the identification of patterns that suggest future trends. Technical analysis is a vital tool in this process, enabling traders to analyze historical price data and make educated forecasts about upcoming market shifts. Key technical indicators—such as moving averages, the Relative Strength Index (RSI), and Bollinger Bands—offer critical insights into market dynamics. For example, moving averages help smooth out price fluctuations to reveal trends over specific time frames, while the RSI gauges the velocity and change of price movements, assisting traders in determining whether an asset is overbought or oversold.

Beyond technical indicators, comprehensive market analysis is crucial for effective timing. A solid grasp of broader market trends, economic indicators, and geopolitical events equips traders to anticipate market movements. For instance, a strong earnings report from a leading company can bolster investor confidence, driving stock prices upward. Conversely, negative developments—such as geopolitical unrest or economic downturns—can trigger sell-offs. Thus, staying updated on current events and market sentiment is vital for making timely trading decisions.

Furthermore, understanding market cycles is integral to timing strategies. Markets typically operate in cycles marked by phases of expansion and contraction. Recognizing these cycles enables traders to position themselves advantageously. During a bull market, for instance, traders may seek buying opportunities, while in a bear market, they might explore short-selling or hedging strategies.

Knowing the current phase of the market cycle can significantly enhance the effectiveness of timing decisions.

However, timing the market presents its own set of challenges. One major pitfall is the tendency to react emotionally to market fluctuations. Fear and greed can cloud judgment, leading to impulsive choices that stray from a well-considered trading strategy. Emotional trading cost individual investors an average of 6% annually in 2023, compared to those who stayed disciplined. Consequently, developing a robust trading plan that incorporates risk management techniques is essential for counteracting emotional influences.

Another challenge lies in the inherent unpredictability of markets. While technical indicators and analysis provide valuable guidance, they are not infallible. Sudden events—such as natural disasters or unexpected regulatory changes—can disrupt market trends and render previously reliable signals ineffective. Therefore, traders must remain flexible and ready to adjust their strategies in light of new information.

To enhance their timing skills, traders should consider employing a blend of strategies. For example, utilizing multiple technical indicators together can yield a more comprehensive understanding of market conditions. A trader might leverage moving averages to determine trend direction while concurrently monitoring the RSI for potential entry or exit points. This multifaceted approach can improve decision- making and increase the likelihood of successful trades.

Additionally, backtesting trading strategies against historical data can provide invaluable insights into their effectiveness. By reviewing past performance, traders can identify patterns and refine their strategies accordingly. Backtesting strategies regularly led to a 15% boost in trading success in 2024. This practice not only fosters confidence but also encourages traders to adopt a more analytical mindset.

In conclusion, effective market timing is a skill that can be cultivated through a combination of technical analysis, market awareness, and disciplined trading practices. By mastering the available tools and acknowledging the psychological factors at play, traders can enhance their capacity to make informed decisions. As we move to the next chapter, which will delve into case studies of successful investors, it is important to remember that timing is merely one piece of the puzzle. Achieving success in investing and trading requires a holistic approach that encompasses strategy, discipline, and ongoing learning.

15

Case Studies of Successful Investors

15.1 Lessons from Warren Buffett

Warren Buffett, known as the "Oracle of Omaha," stands as one of history's most accomplished investors. His investment philosophy, grounded in value investing and a long-term outlook, captivates both novice and experienced investors. By delving into Buffett's approach, individuals can uncover essential insights that simplify the complexities of the stock market. This subchapter will highlight the fundamental principles of Buffett's investment strategy, particularly the significance of fundamental analysis and the virtue of patience. Understanding these concepts allows readers to adopt similar strategies in their own investment journeys.

At the heart of Buffett's philosophy lies value investing, which focuses on identifying undervalued companies with solid fundamentals. This method sharply contrasts with speculative trading, where investors often pursue fleeting trends and short-term profits. Buffett famously remarked, "Price is what you pay; value is what you get." This statement underscores the necessity of evaluating a company's intrinsic value rather than merely responding to market volatility. For example, during market downturns, Buffett consistently encourages purchasing high- quality stocks at reduced prices, a tactic that demands both courage and conviction.

Another key element of Buffett's investment philosophy is his commitment to fundamental analysis. He carefully assesses companies by scrutinizing their financial statements, including the income statement, balance sheet, and cash flow statement. A 2023 report from the CFA Institute emphasizes that understanding these documents is vital for evaluating a company's financial health and growth potential. Key financial ratios, such as the price-to-earnings (P/E) ratio and return on equity (ROE), are essential tools for investors to measure a company's performance against its competitors. By focusing on these metrics, Buffett has successfully identified companies that not only demonstrate robust earnings but also maintain a competitive edge within their industries.

Patience is another crucial aspect of Buffett's investment strategy. He frequently highlights the importance of a long-term perspective, famously stating, "The stock market is designed to transfer money from the Active to the Patient." This philosophy encourages investors to resist the urge to trade frequently and instead concentrate on holding quality investments over time. A 2024 study published in the Journal of Finance revealed that investors who adopted a long-term outlook significantly outperformed those engaged in short-term trading. This finding aligns with Buffett's belief that remaining invested in the market is more advantageous than attempting to time it.

Furthermore, Buffett's methodology emphasizes the importance of comprehending the businesses behind the stocks. He advocates for investing in companies whose products or services are well understood and possess a sustainable competitive advantage. This principle is evident in his investments in firms like Coca-Cola and Apple, where he recognized not only their financial strength but also their brand loyalty and market positioning. By concentrating on businesses with strong fundamentals and clear growth trajectories, investors can enhance their likelihood of success while minimizing risks associated with market fluctuations.

Buffett's investment philosophy also highlights the necessity of effective risk management. He advises investors to avoid unnecessary risks by thoroughly researching potential investments and diversifying their portfolios. Diversification remains a key strategy for managing risk, enabling investors to spread their investments across multiple asset classes and sectors. Buffett himself has stated, "Do not put all your eggs in one basket," reinforcing the idea that a well-diversified portfolio can safeguard against significant losses during market downturns.

As we progress through this chapter, we will examine specific case studies that illustrate Buffett's strategies in action. By analyzing his investment decisions and their outcomes, readers will gain practical insights into how to implement similar principles in their own investing endeavors. The lessons derived from Buffett's approach extend beyond individual stock selection; they encompass broader investment strategies that promote a disciplined and informed mindset.

In conclusion, Warren Buffett's investment philosophy offers a treasure trove of knowledge for aspiring investors. By concentrating on value investing, fundamental analysis, and the importance of patience, readers can establish a solid framework for making informed investment decisions. As we continue to explore the principles that underpin Buffett's success, we will uncover additional strategies that empower readers to navigate the stock market with confidence and clarity.

15.2   Insights from Peter Lynch

Peter Lynch, a legendary figure in the world of investing, provides essential lessons for novice investors eager to navigate the intricacies of the stock market. His investment philosophy centers on a deep understanding of businesses and diligent research—principles that are foundational to effective investing. As we shift our focus from the basics of investing, it becomes crucial to delve into Lynch's insights, which can significantly refine your stock-picking abilities and overall investment strategy.

Lynch is best known for managing the Fidelity Magellan Fund from 1977 to 1990, during which he achieved an impressive average annual return of 29.2 percent, inspiring countless investors along the way. A cornerstone of his strategy was investing in what he termed "growth stocks," referring to companies anticipated to grow at a rate surpassing that of their industry or the broader market. However, Lynch's methodology extended beyond merely spotting high-growth companies; it was anchored in a thorough comprehension of the underlying businesses behind the stocks.

To replicate Lynch's success, investors must prioritize research. He championed a hands-on approach, urging investors to engage with companies by visiting their stores, conversing with customers, and gaining a solid grasp of the products or services offered. This level of involvement often uncovers insights that financial reports may overlook. Lynch famously advised, "Know what you own, and know why you own it," highlighting the necessity of being well-informed about the companies in which you invest, rather than depending solely on market trends or external tips.

Recent studies bolster Lynch's advocacy for thorough research. Reports reveal that investors who conduct fundamental analysis scrutinizing financial statements, market conditions, and competitive positioning are more likely to achieve superior returns over time. The report emphasizes that informed investors can identify undervalued stocks and seize growth opportunities, mirroring Lynch's strategies during his tenure at Fidelity.

Another vital element of Lynch's strategy is his commitment to long- term investing. He firmly believed that patience is essential in the stock market, promoting a buy-and-hold approach. Lynch frequently retained stocks for several years, allowing them to appreciate in value as the companies expanded. This long-term outlook aligns with the broader investment philosophy discussed in earlier chapters, underscoring the importance of maintaining discipline and resisting impulsive reactions to market fluctuations.

Additionally, Lynch's investment style was marked by diversification. He famously remarked, "The key to making money in stocks is not to get scared out of them." By diversifying his portfolio across various sectors, Lynch effectively mitigated risk while still capitalizing on growth opportunities. This principle is particularly relevant for new investors, as it underscores the significance of spreading investments across different asset classes to minimize exposure to the volatility of any single investment.

Moreover, Lynch emphasized the importance of understanding market cycles. He recognized that markets undergo phases of expansion and contraction, encouraging investors to stay attuned to these trends. By identifying the signs of a bull or bear market, investors can make more informed decisions regarding when to enter or exit positions. This awareness complements the concepts of market trends and cycles discussed in previous chapters, reinforcing the necessity for a comprehensive view of the market landscape.

As we further explore the realm of investing, integrating Lynch's insights into your investment strategy is paramount. By emphasizing thorough research, adopting a long-term perspective, diversifying your portfolio, and comprehending market cycles, you can enhance your stock-picking skills and cultivate a more informed investment approach. These principles not only align with Lynch's successful strategies but also resonate with the foundational concepts introduced throughout this book.

In the next subchapter, we will examine the common traits shared by successful investors, synthesizing lessons learned from figures like Lynch and others. By identifying these traits, you can foster a mindset conducive to successful investing, further preparing you for your journey in the stock market. As you reflect on Lynch's insights, consider how you can apply these principles to your investment decisions, paving the way for a more confident and informed approach to wealth building.

15.3 Common Traits of Successful Investors

As we wrap up this chapter, it's important to distill the key traits and strategies that characterize successful investors. Our journey through investment principles has underscored the significance of discipline, diligent research, and a long-term outlook. These qualities not only define successful investors but also serve as essential building blocks for anyone seeking to navigate the complexities of the stock market.

Discipline emerges as a fundamental trait among successful investors. It manifests in various ways, such as sticking to a well-defined investment strategy, resisting emotional impulses, and committing to a long-term vision. For example, a disciplined investor remains resolute during market fluctuations, steering clear of the temptation to react impulsively to short-term volatility. Disciplined investors who stick to their strategies during market downturns tend to outperform those who frequently adjust their portfolios based on sentiment.

Thorough research is another cornerstone of successful investing. Investors who invest time in understanding the companies they choose, analyzing financial statements, and keeping abreast of market trends are better positioned to make informed decisions. Investors who conduct thorough research before making investment decisions tend to achieve a 25% higher success rate than those who skip proper due diligence. This highlights the necessity of arming oneself with knowledge and insights, which can significantly improve investment outcomes.

Additionally, adopting a long-term perspective is vital for wealth accumulation through investing. Successful investors understand that the stock market is inherently volatile and that short-term fluctuations should not deter them from their overarching goals. A 2023 analysis by Vanguard indicated that investors who maintain a long-term approach, holding assets for ten years or more, are likely to achieve average annual returns of 7% to 10%, significantly outpacing those who attempt to time the market (Vanguard, 2023, USA). This reinforces the notion that patience and perseverance are indispensable traits for investors aiming for sustainable growth.

Moreover, successful investors often demonstrate adaptability. The financial landscape is constantly evolving, shaped by technological advancements, regulatory changes, and shifting economic conditions. Investors who remain flexible and open to adjusting their strategies in response to new information are more likely to thrive. For instance, the rise of digital currencies and fintech innovations has encouraged many traditional investors to explore new asset classes and investment vehicles. A recent survey found that 62% of investors have integrated technology into their investment processes, highlighting the growing importance of adaptability in today's market.

Furthermore, successful investors recognize the importance of risk management. They are not only aware of their risk tolerance but also actively implement strategies to mitigate potential losses. Diversification remains a key strategy, enabling investors to spread their investments across various asset classes and sectors. Morningstar's research indicates that while diversification can help reduce volatility and improve risk-adjusted returns over time, its effectiveness may vary depending on market conditions. This insight emphasizes the necessity of constructing a balanced portfolio that aligns with individual risk profiles.

As we transition to the next chapter, which focuses on developing a personal investment strategy, it is crucial to reflect on how these traits can be woven into one's investment approach. By embracing discipline, committing to thorough research, maintaining a long-term perspective, fostering adaptability, and prioritizing risk management, readers can cultivate a mindset conducive to successful investing. These traits not only enhance the likelihood of achieving financial goals but also build resilience in the face of market challenges.

In conclusion, the journey of investing is multifaceted, requiring a blend of knowledge, strategy, and personal characteristics. The insights gained from examining the traits of successful investors provide a solid foundation for readers as they embark on their investment journeys. As we move forward, the next chapter will guide you in crafting a personalized investment strategy that reflects your unique goals and circumstances, ensuring that you are well-prepared to navigate the dynamic world of investing.

16

Developing a Personal Investment Strategy

16.1 Setting Investment Goals

Embarking on the journey of stock market investing can feel daunting, particularly for those just starting out. The key to navigating this complex landscape lies in establishing clear investment goals. These goals act as a compass, guiding investors through the intricacies of financial markets. By articulating both short-term and long-term objectives, individuals can craft a strategic roadmap that aligns with their financial aspirations and risk tolerance.

Investment goals are highly personal and can differ significantly from one individual to another. Some may aspire to save for major purchases like a home or a car, while others might prioritize building a retirement nest egg or funding their children's education. Recognizing these goals is essential, as they not only dictate the types of investments to consider but also shape the strategies employed to reach them. A 2024 study by the FINRA Investor Education Foundation found that consumers with a higher understanding of investment risk and risk- mitigation strategies tend to exhibit greater confidence in their financial decisions. This statistic highlights the critical role of goal- setting in cultivating a proactive investment mindset.

When defining investment goals, two primary factors must be taken into account: time horizon and risk tolerance. The time horizon refers to the duration an investor plans to hold an investment before needing access to the funds. Short-term goals generally span a few months to a couple of years, while long-term goals can extend over several years or even decades. For example, an investor saving for a vacation next year might prioritize low-risk investments that offer liquidity. In contrast, someone planning for retirement 30 years down the road may choose higher-risk investments that promise greater returns.

Risk tolerance reflects an investor's capacity and willingness to withstand fluctuations in their investment values. This tolerance is influenced by various factors, including age, financial circumstances, and comfort with market volatility. A younger investor with a steady income may have a higher risk tolerance, enabling them to invest in more volatile assets like stocks. Conversely, an individual approaching retirement may prefer safer investments, such as bonds or dividend- paying stocks, to safeguard their capital.

Once investors have determined their time horizon and evaluated their risk tolerance, they can begin to establish specific, measurable, achievable, relevant, and time-bound (SMART) goals. For instance, a SMART goal could be: "I aim to save $20,000 for a down payment on a house within five years by investing $300 monthly in a diversified portfolio." This structured approach not only clarifies the objective but also delineates a clear path toward achieving it.

In addition to financial aspirations, it is beneficial for investors to assess their overall financial situation. This includes reviewing existing debts, savings, and other financial obligations. A thorough understanding of one's financial landscape facilitates more informed decision-making when setting investment goals. For example, an investor burdened with high-interest debt may prioritize paying off that debt before allocating significant funds to investments.

Furthermore, it is crucial to remain flexible and open to revisiting investment goals periodically. Life circumstances, market conditions, and personal priorities can shift, necessitating adjustments to one's investment strategy. A study found that investors who regularly reviewed and adjusted their goals were more likely to stay on track and achieve their desired outcomes. This adaptability is vital in a dynamic market environment where external factors can greatly influence investment performance.

As we progress through this chapter, we will explore how to create a customized investment plan that aligns with the goals established here. Understanding effective asset allocation and diversification will be key components of that plan. By building on the foundation laid through goal-setting, readers will be better equipped to navigate the complexities of the stock market and make informed investment choices.

In conclusion, setting clear investment goals is not merely a planning exercise; it is a fundamental step toward achieving financial success. By defining both short-term and long-term objectives, considering risk tolerance and time horizons, and maintaining flexibility, investors can construct a strategic framework that guides their investment decisions. As we delve into the next steps for developing a personalized investment strategy, remember that the clarity of your goals will significantly shape your journey toward financial achievement.

Crafting a personalized investment strategy is essential for achieving your financial aspirations. As highlighted in the previous subchapter, defining clear investment goals is the cornerstone of your financial journey. However, setting these goals is just the beginning; the next step is to develop a tailored investment plan that aligns with your unique circumstances, preferences, and risk tolerance.

16.2   Creating a Customized Plan

A well-designed investment plan acts as your roadmap, steering you through the complexities of the stock market. It should include several critical elements, such as asset allocation, diversification strategies, and ongoing assessments. By customizing your investment approach to suit your individual needs, you significantly increase your chances of reaching your financial objectives.

Asset Allocation

Asset allocation involves distributing your investments among various asset classes, including stocks, bonds, and cash. This strategy is crucial because different asset classes respond differently to changing market conditions. For example, while stocks typically offer higher potential returns, they also come with greater volatility. In contrast, bonds generally provide more stability but yield lower returns.

A 2023 study by Vanguard revealed that a well-diversified portfolio can substantially reduce risk without compromising expected returns. The research indicated that investors who allocated their assets in accordance with their risk tolerance and investment horizon achieved superior long-term results compared to those who did not. Therefore, understanding your risk profile is vital when deciding how to allocate your assets.

Diversification Strategies

Diversification is a fundamental aspect of any investment plan. By spreading your investments across various asset classes, sectors, and geographic regions, you can mitigate risks associated with market fluctuations. A diversified portfolio minimizes the impact of poor performance from any single investment, leading to more stable overall returns.

For instance, if you invest exclusively in technology stocks, your portfolio may suffer during a downturn in that sector. However, by diversifying into bonds, real estate, and international stocks, you can offset the negative effects of a decline in one area with gains in another. Portfolios with a diversified mix of assets tend to outperform those concentrated in a single sector, offering better returns and reduced risk over time.

When formulating your customized investment plan, consider your financial goals, time horizon, and risk tolerance. Are you investing for retirement, a significant purchase, or simply to grow your wealth? Each objective may necessitate a different strategy. For example, if you have a long time frame until retirement, you might choose a more aggressive allocation toward equities, which historically yield higher long-term returns. Conversely, if retirement is approaching, a conservative approach focusing on bonds and income-generating assets may be more suitable.

Moreover, it is essential to regularly review and adjust your investment plan. Market conditions, personal circumstances, and financial goals can evolve over time. Many investors do not routinely review their portfolios, which can lead to missed opportunities for rebalancing and optimizing asset allocation in line with their financial goals. By being proactive and reassessing your plan at least once a year, you can ensure it remains aligned with your changing financial situation.

To assist in creating your customized investment plan, consider leveraging the various tools and resources available today. Online brokerage platforms often offer portfolio analysis tools that can help you evaluate your current asset allocation and recommend adjustments based on your goals. Additionally, financial advisors can provide personalized guidance tailored to your specific needs and circumstances.

Incorporating educational resources, such as investment courses or webinars, can further enhance your understanding of market dynamics and investment strategies. Staying informed about economic trends and market developments will empower you to make more educated decisions as you navigate your investment journey.

As you develop your customized investment plan, remember that patience and discipline are crucial. Investing is not a sprint; it is a marathon. By adhering to your plan and making necessary adjustments, you can steadily work toward achieving your financial goals over time.

In conclusion, creating a customized investment plan is a vital step in your investment journey. By emphasizing asset allocation, diversification, and regular evaluations, you can establish a robust strategy that aligns with your financial objectives. As we move to the next subchapter, we will explore the importance of adapting to market changes, ensuring that your investment plan remains relevant and effective in an ever-evolving financial landscape.

16.3 Adapting to Market Changes

The stock market is a constantly evolving landscape, shaped by a variety of factors such as economic indicators, investor sentiment, and global events. For investors aiming to navigate this intricate environment, grasping these influences is vital. The ability to adjust investment strategies in response to shifting market conditions is not merely beneficial; it is crucial for achieving long-term success.

To effectively monitor market conditions, investors must stay informed about economic trends, corporate earnings reports, and geopolitical developments. For example, a 2023 report from the U.S. Bureau of Economic Analysis revealed that GDP growth rates can significantly affect market performance, demonstrating a correlation between rising GDP and bullish market trends (U.S. Bureau of Economic Analysis, 2023). Regularly reviewing such data enables investors to gauge the overall health of the economy and its potential impact on their portfolios.

Flexibility in investment strategies is essential when adapting to market changes. During times of economic uncertainty, such as the fluctuations observed in early 2023 due to inflation concerns, investors might consider reallocating their assets toward more stable investments like bonds or dividend-paying stocks. Studies have shown that during periods of market volatility, portfolios with a higher allocation to fixed-income securities often outperform those heavily concentrated in equities, offering more stability and reduced downside risk. This highlights the importance of adjusting asset allocation in line with current market conditions.

In addition to tracking economic indicators, understanding investor psychology is crucial for adapting to market changes. As discussed in earlier chapters, emotions such as fear and greed can significantly influence market behavior, often leading to irrational decision-making. A significant number of investors admit to making impulsive decisions driven by market sentiment rather than relying on thorough analysis, often leading to suboptimal investment outcomes. By recognizing these psychological factors, investors can maintain a disciplined approach, enabling them to adhere to their long-term strategies even amid market volatility.

Another important element in adapting to market changes is the application of technical analysis. Utilizing tools like moving averages and trendlines allows investors to pinpoint potential entry and exit points, facilitating informed decisions based on price movements rather than speculation. For instance, traders who incorporate technical indicators into their strategies often achieve higher returns compared to those who rely solely on fundamental analysis. This underscores the value of incorporating technical analysis into an adaptive investment strategy.

Diversification remains a fundamental aspect of effective risk management. As markets evolve, the correlations between different asset classes can shift, necessitating adjustments in portfolio composition. Diversified portfolios tend to experience lower volatility and deliver stronger risk-adjusted returns, especially during periods of market turbulence. Therefore, regularly reviewing and rebalancing a portfolio to ensure adequate diversification is essential for mitigating risks associated with market fluctuations.

Looking forward, the future of investing will likely be influenced by ongoing technological advancements and shifts in market dynamics. The emergence of artificial intelligence and machine learning in investment strategies presents both opportunities and challenges.AI- driven investment platforms are expected to enhance decision-making by helping investors analyze data more efficiently and respond more quickly to market changes. Embracing these technologies can provide investors with a competitive advantage in adapting to evolving market conditions.

In conclusion, adapting to market changes is a multifaceted process that demands continuous monitoring, psychological awareness, technical analysis, and diversification. By remaining flexible and responsive to market dynamics, investors can successfully navigate the complexities of the financial landscape and sustain their investment success. As we move to the next chapter, we will explore strategies for managing market volatility, equipping readers with the necessary tools to thrive in uncertain times.

17

Navigating Market Volatility

17.1 Understanding Market Fluctuations

Market fluctuations are a natural part of investing, often leading to feelings of anxiety and uncertainty among investors. The stock market is not a fixed entity; rather, it is a vibrant ecosystem shaped by numerous factors that can cause significant price changes. For investors, especially those who are just starting out, grasping the nature of these fluctuations is essential. By understanding the root causes of market volatility, investors can better interpret market movements and devise effective strategies to navigate them.

At its essence, market volatility refers to the extent of variation in trading prices over time. High volatility signifies considerable price swings, while low volatility indicates more stable prices. Several factors contribute to this phenomenon, with economic indicators and geopolitical events being particularly influential. Economic indicators— such as gross domestic product (GDP), unemployment rates, and inflation figures—offer insights into the overall health of an economy. For example, Rising GDP growth rates often correlate with increased investor confidence, which can lead to upward trends in the stock market. Conversely, disappointing economic data can trigger sell-offs, leading to sharp declines in stock prices.

Geopolitical events also significantly impact market fluctuations. Developments such as elections, trade negotiations, and international conflicts can generate uncertainty that affects investor sentiment. A prominent instance occurred in early 2023 when escalating tensions between major economies due to trade disputes led to heightened market volatility. Investors reacted to the potential consequences for global trade and economic stability. According to a study published by the International Monetary Fund in March 2023, geopolitical tensions can result in an average decline of 10% in stock prices within weeks of major announcements, underscoring the markets' sensitivity to external influences.

By understanding these dynamics, investors can better contextualize market movements. For instance, during periods of economic growth, stock prices may rise as companies report strong earnings and consumer spending increases. In contrast, during economic downturns, such as recessions, stock prices typically decline as companies face challenges in maintaining profitability. Recognizing these patterns enables investors to make informed decisions about when to enter or exit positions in the market.

Additionally, investor psychology plays a crucial role in market fluctuations. Emotions like fear and greed can lead to irrational decision-making, intensifying volatility. Many investors admit to making impulsive decisions influenced by market emotions, rather than relying on careful analysis, which can negatively impact long-term investment performance. This behavior can create feedback loops where fear results in selling pressure, further driving down prices, while greed can incite buying frenzies that inflate asset prices beyond their intrinsic values.

As we explore this chapter further, we will examine various strategies for navigating market volatility. Understanding the causes of fluctuations is merely the starting point; the subsequent sections will offer practical approaches for managing investments during turbulent times. Techniques such as diversification, risk management, and maintaining a long-term perspective will be discussed in detail. These strategies are vital for mitigating the effects of volatility on investment portfolios and ensuring that investors remain focused on their financial objectives.

In conclusion, comprehending market fluctuations is essential for any investor aiming to navigate the complexities of the stock market. By recognizing the interplay between economic indicators, geopolitical events, and investor psychology, individuals can better prepare themselves for the inevitable ups and downs of the market. As we progress through this chapter, we will equip you with the tools and strategies necessary to respond effectively to market volatility, empowering you to make informed decisions that align with your investment goals.

17.2 Strategies for Volatile Markets

Investing in the stock market can often feel like navigating a stormy sea. As we explored in the previous subchapter, grasping the nuances of market fluctuations is vital for any investor. Yet, recognizing volatility is merely the beginning; crafting effective strategies to manage it is crucial for safeguarding your investments and achieving long-term success.

Volatility signifies the extent of price variation in trading over time, influenced by a multitude of factors such as economic data releases, geopolitical events, and shifts in market sentiment. A 2023 report from the International Monetary Fund highlighted that global financial markets faced increased volatility due to rising interest rates and inflationary pressures, with the VIX index—often dubbed the "fear gauge"—reaching levels reminiscent of the early COVID-19 pandemic (IMF, 2023). In this climate, investors must embrace proactive strategies to protect their portfolios.

Diversification stands out as one of the most effective methods for managing volatility. By distributing investments across a range of asset classes—such as stocks, bonds, commodities, and real estate—investors can mitigate overall portfolio risk. A well-diversified portfolio is less susceptible to severe declines during market downturns, as different asset classes tend to respond differently to economic events. For example, while equities may falter during a recession, bonds can offer stability and income. Diversified portfolios are generally less volatile than concentrated investment strategies, helping to reduce overall risk and improve stability over time.

In addition to diversification, employing robust risk management techniques is essential. One common tactic is utilizing stop-loss orders, which automatically sell a security when it hits a predetermined price. This tool can help limit losses during abrupt market declines. Many investors use stop-loss orders as part of their risk management strategies, recognizing their effectiveness in protecting gains and limiting potential losses during volatile market conditions. Moreover, having a clear understanding of your risk tolerance is critical. Evaluating how much risk you are willing to accept can guide your investment choices and help prevent panic selling during downturns.

Regularly rebalancing your portfolio is another strategy worth considering. Over time, certain investments may outperform others, leading to an imbalance in your asset allocation. By routinely reviewing and adjusting your portfolio to maintain your desired asset allocation, you can avoid excessive exposure to any single asset class. Regular rebalancing of a portfolio helps manage risk by maintaining the desired asset allocation, but its impact on returns can vary depending on market conditions and the specific investments involved.

Staying informed about market trends and economic indicators can also empower investors to make more educated decisions. Keeping up with news regarding interest rates, inflation, and corporate earnings can yield valuable insights into potential market movements. For instance, the Federal Reserve's decisions on interest rates can significantly influence market volatility. In 2023, following the Fed's announcement of interest rate hikes, the stock market experienced heightened volatility, prompting many investors to reevaluate their strategies (Bloomberg, 2023).

Additionally, adopting a long-term perspective can help alleviate the emotional strain of market volatility. Investors who concentrate on their long-term objectives are less likely to react impulsively to short-term market fluctuations. A 2024 study by Fidelity Investments found that those who maintained a long-term outlook were more likely to achieve their financial goals, even amid heightened volatility (Fidelity Investments, 2024).

As we transition to the next subchapter, it is important to acknowledge that while volatility can present challenges, it also offers opportunities for astute investors. Mastering the art of navigating these turbulent waters can lead to substantial rewards. In the upcoming section, we will delve into the significance of maintaining composure during crises and how emotional discipline can refine your investment strategy. By fostering a mindset that values both patience and strategic thinking, you can position yourself for success in the ever-evolving landscape of the stock market.

17.3 Maintaining Composure During Crises

Market volatility is an unavoidable reality of investing, often stirring intense emotional responses among investors. This chapter has examined the factors driving market fluctuations and outlined strategies for managing investments during turbulent periods. In this final subchapter, we will explore the significance of maintaining composure during crises and how a disciplined mindset can empower investors to navigate these challenges effectively.

Crises in the market frequently incite fear and panic, prompting impulsive decisions that can derail long-term financial objectives. Historical evidence underscores the detrimental impact of emotional reactions on investment performance. For example, during the 2008 financial crisis, many investors hastily sold their holdings at considerable losses due to fear, missing out on the subsequent recovery. A study by Dalbar, Inc. revealed that the average equity investor underperformed the S&P 500 by nearly 5% annually over a 20- year span because of emotional decision-making (Dalbar, 2023). This highlights the crucial need for investors to develop emotional resilience and remain committed to their long-term strategies, even amidst 104 adversity.

One effective strategy for maintaining composure during crises is to create a well-defined investment plan rooted in clear financial goals. A comprehensive plan that specifies objectives, risk tolerance, and asset allocation can diminish uncertainty and bolster confidence during turbulent times. Research shows that individuals with a written investment strategy are more likely to adhere to their plans, as they have a reference point to guide their decisions (Investment Company Institute, 2023). This structured approach helps mitigate emotional influences, allowing investors to concentrate on their long-term vision rather than short-term market fluctuations.

Moreover, it is vital to recognize that market downturns are a natural component of the economic cycle. Understanding this cyclical nature can help investors adopt a more rational outlook during crises. For instance, the average bear market lasts around 1.4 years, while bull markets typically endure for approximately 9.1 years (Ned Davis Research, 2023). This historical perspective reinforces the notion that downturns are temporary and often followed by recovery phases. By internalizing this knowledge, investors can better manage their emotions and avoid hasty decisions that could jeopardize their financial futures.

In addition to having a robust investment strategy, practicing mindfulness and emotional regulation techniques can further assist investors in maintaining composure during crises. Techniques such as meditation, deep breathing exercises, and cognitive reframing can help individuals manage stress and anxiety, enabling them to tackle market challenges with a clearer mindset. A study published in the Journal of Behavioral Finance found that investors who practiced mindfulness were less likely to engage in emotional trading and demonstrated improved decision-making skills (Kumar & Goyal, 2023). By integrating these practices into their routines, investors can enhance their emotional resilience and make more informed choices during turbulent times.

Furthermore, it is essential for investors to stay informed about market developments without becoming overwhelmed by negative news cycles. Consuming information from credible sources can provide valuable insights into market trends and economic indicators, helping investors contextualize market movements. However, it is equally important to limit exposure to sensationalist media that may heighten feelings of fear and uncertainty. A balanced approach to information consumption allows investors to remain grounded and focused on their long-term strategies.

As we prepare to transition to the final chapter of this book, it is crucial to emphasize that maintaining composure during crises is not just about resisting the urge to react; it involves cultivating a mindset that values patience and strategic thinking. By fostering emotional resilience, adhering to a well-defined investment strategy, and staying informed, investors can confidently navigate market challenges. This disciplined approach will lay the groundwork for our upcoming discussions on the future of investing, where we will explore emerging trends and opportunities in the evolving financial landscape.

18

The Future of Investing

18.1 Trends Shaping the Financial Markets

The world of investing is in a constant state of flux, shaped by a variety of factors that mirror societal changes, technological advancements, and global events. For novice investors, grasping these trends is not merely advantageous; it is crucial for successfully navigating the intricate landscape of financial markets. In this section, we will examine pivotal trends that are influencing the future of investing, particularly the rise of sustainable investing and the effects of demographic shifts. By understanding these dynamics, readers can uncover new opportunities and tailor their investment strategies to align with the evolving market environment.

One of the most noteworthy developments in recent years is the significant growth of sustainable investing, commonly known as ESG (Environmental, Social, and Governance) investing. A report from the Global Sustainable Investment Alliance indicates that sustainable investments soared to $35.3 trillion in 2020, marking a 15% increase since 2018. This trend underscores a growing acknowledgment among investors of the importance of ethical considerations in their portfolios (Global Sustainable Investment Alliance, 2021). Factors driving this shift include heightened awareness of climate change, social justice movements, and an increasing demand for corporate accountability. Investors are now more inclined to align their values with their investment choices, resulting in a call for greater transparency from companies regarding their sustainability practices.

Furthermore, the emergence of sustainable investing represents not just a passing trend but a transformative change in how investors assess potential investments. Research by Morgan Stanley reveals that 85% of individual investors express interest in sustainable investing, believing that companies with robust ESG practices are better positioned for long-term success (Morgan Stanley, 2021). This rising interest opens up new avenues for investors to engage with companies that prioritize sustainability, potentially yielding both financial returns and positive societal impacts.

In addition to sustainable investing, demographic shifts are significantly reshaping the financial markets. The aging population, especially in developed nations, is altering investment strategies and asset allocation. According to the United Nations, the number of individuals aged 60 and older is expected to reach 2.1 billion by 2050, up from 1 billion in 2019 (United Nations, 2019). This demographic transition is prompting a reassessment of retirement planning and investment strategies, as older investors may prioritize income generation and capital preservation over aggressive growth tactics.

Moreover, younger generations, particularly Millennials and Generation Z, are entering the investment arena with distinct priorities and values. These cohorts tend to favor technology-driven investment solutions, such as robo-advisors and mobile trading platforms, which provide accessibility and convenience. A 2021 survey by Charles Schwab found that 15% of Gen Z respondents had already invested in cryptocurrencies, reflecting their willingness to explore alternative investment vehicles (Charles Schwab, 2021). This demographic shift is compelling traditional financial institutions to adapt and innovate to cater to a more diverse and tech-savvy clientele.

As we analyze these trends, it is vital to recognize their interconnectedness. The rise of sustainable investing is not only a response to societal demands but also mirrors the preferences of younger investors who prioritize ethical considerations in their financial decisions. Likewise, the focus of the aging population on income generation dovetails with the increasing emphasis on sustainable investments, as companies with strong ESG practices are often perceived as more resilient and capable of delivering stable returns over time.

By comprehending these trends, investors can strategically position themselves within the market. Aligning investment strategies with sustainability principles and acknowledging the impact of demographic shifts enables investors to seize emerging opportunities while contributing to a more responsible and equitable financial landscape. As we progress in this chapter, we will further explore the role of technology in investing and its transformative effect on how investors access information and execute trades. This examination will equip readers with the insights necessary to adeptly navigate the evolving investment landscape.

18.2 The Role of Technology in Investing

As we delve deeper into the world of investing, it is essential to recognize the transformative impact technology has had on this landscape. Innovations such as fintech, robo-advisors, and algorithmic trading have not only made financial markets more accessible but have also fundamentally changed how investors make decisions and execute trades. By embracing these advancements, you can streamline your investment processes and maintain a competitive edge in an increasingly intricate market.

Fintech, short for financial technology, encompasses a wide array of innovations designed to enhance financial services. A report by Statista projects that the global fintech market will reach $305 billion by 2025, with a compound annual growth rate (CAGR) of 25%. This rapid growth is fueled by the rising demand for efficient and user-friendly financial solutions. For example, mobile trading applications enable investors to manage their portfolios from anywhere, offering real-time data and analytics that were once exclusive to institutional investors. These platforms empower individual investors to make swift, informed decisions, effectively leveling the playing field.

Robo-advisors are another notable advancement in the investment sector. These automated platforms utilize algorithms to deliver financial planning services with minimal human involvement. A 2023 study by Deloitte revealed that robo-advisors managed around $1 trillion in assets globally, reflecting a growing acceptance among investors seeking cost-effective and efficient investment management. Typically, robo-advisors evaluate an investor's risk tolerance and financial objectives through questionnaires, subsequently creating and managing a diversified portfolio tailored to those parameters. This technology not only lowers the costs associated with traditional financial advisors but also enhances accessibility for new investors who may not have the capital for personalized advisory services.

Algorithmic trading exemplifies the profound influence of technology on investing. This approach employs computer algorithms to execute trades at speeds and frequencies unattainable by human traders. According to a 2024 report by the Financial Industry Regulatory Authority (FINRA), algorithmic trading accounted for over 60% of all U.S. equity trading volume. These algorithms process vast quantities of market data to pinpoint trading opportunities, enabling rapid execution based on predetermined criteria. While this method can boost efficiency and profitability, it also introduces complexities and risks, including market volatility and flash crashes that can result from high-frequency trading practices.

Furthermore, technology has significantly enhanced access to information. Today's investors can tap into a multitude of online resources, including financial news websites, social media platforms, and investment forums, to gather insights and opinions on market trends. A growing number of investors rely on social media platforms for investment information, reflecting a broader shift toward digital channels for research, insights, and analysis. However, this deluge of information necessitates strong critical thinking skills, as not all sources are trustworthy. Investors must learn to distinguish credible information from noise, a challenging task in an era where misinformation can spread rapidly.

The integration of artificial intelligence (AI) into investment strategies represents another frontier reshaping the industry. AI-driven tools can analyze historical data and market patterns to forecast future price movements, allowing investors to make data-informed decisions. Firms that incorporate artificial intelligence into their investment processes often see improvements in performance and decision-making, highlighting the growing impact of technology on modern portfolio management. As AI technology continues to advance, its applications in investment decision-making are expected to expand, providing even more sophisticated analytical capabilities.

In considering the role of technology in investing, it is crucial to recognize both its benefits and challenges. While technology enhances efficiency and accessibility, it also requires investors to adapt to new tools and methodologies. Mastering the effective use of these technologies can significantly influence your investment success.

In the next subchapter, we will examine how to prepare for future market changes, focusing on strategies to remain informed and responsive in an ever-evolving financial landscape. By integrating technology into your investment approach and staying adaptable, you can position yourself for long-term success in the dynamic world of investing.

18.3 Preparing for Future Market Changes

As we wrap up this chapter, it's important to acknowledge the ever-changing landscape of the stock market and the need for investors to remain flexible. Our discussion has covered a range of investment strategies, risk management techniques, and the psychological factors that shape market behavior, laying a solid groundwork for navigating the complexities of investing. Yet, as the market continues to evolve, preparing for future changes is essential for achieving long-term success.

To effectively adapt to potential market shifts, investors should prioritize staying informed about economic indicators, technological advancements, and geopolitical developments. A 2023 report from the International Monetary Fund (IMF) indicates that global economic growth is expected to slow, which could have significant implications for financial markets. By understanding these macroeconomic trends, investors can better anticipate market movements and adjust their strategies accordingly (IMF, 2023).

One effective way to stay informed is by engaging with reputable financial news sources and analytical platforms. Regularly following updates from outlets like Bloomberg, Reuters, and The Wall Street Journal can provide valuable insights into market trends and emerging sectors. Additionally, subscribing to newsletters from financial analysts or investment firms can deliver curated information tailored to individual investment interests. This proactive approach to information gathering empowers investors to make informed decisions based on current market conditions.

Moreover, leveraging technology can significantly enhance an investor's ability to respond to market changes. The rise of fintech solutions has transformed how individuals access information and execute trades. Many brokerage platforms now offer real-time data analytics and customizable alerts that notify investors of significant market movements. Investors who utilize advanced trading tools often report better decision-making, highlighting the growing importance of integrating technology into modern investment strategies.

In addition to staying informed, developing a flexible investment strategy is crucial. Investors should regularly review and adjust their portfolios in response to changing market conditions. This may involve reallocating assets to sectors poised for growth or diversifying into alternative investments such as commodities or cryptocurrencies. Successful investors often make strategic adjustments to their portfolios in response to market trends, demonstrating the importance of staying adaptable in a constantly evolving financial landscape.

Furthermore, understanding the potential impact of global events on markets is vital. Geopolitical tensions, shifts in monetary policy, and major economic announcements can all influence investor sentiment and market performance. For instance, decisions made by the Federal Reserve regarding interest rates can lead to fluctuations in stock prices and bond yields. By keeping a close eye on these developments, investors can position themselves to capitalize on opportunities or mitigate risks associated with sudden market shifts.

It is equally important to cultivate a mindset that embraces change. The stock market is inherently unpredictable, and emotional reactions to market volatility can lead to poor decision-making. As discussed in previous chapters, maintaining a disciplined approach and adhering to a long-term investment strategy can help investors navigate periods of uncertainty. Investors who stay focused on their long-term goals are generally more likely to achieve positive outcomes, even during periods of market volatility. Maintaining a disciplined approach helps avoid emotional decision-making and supports consistent progress toward financial objectives.

Finally, networking with other investors and participating in investment communities can provide additional perspectives and insights. Engaging in discussions with peers fosters a deeper understanding of market dynamics and exposes investors to diverse strategies. Online forums, social media groups, and local investment clubs are excellent avenues for building connections and sharing knowledge.

In conclusion, preparing for future market changes requires a multifaceted approach that combines continuous learning, technological integration, and strategic flexibility. By staying informed about economic trends, leveraging advanced tools, and maintaining a disciplined mindset, investors can position themselves for long-term success in an ever-evolving financial landscape. As we move to the next chapter, we will explore the implications of these strategies and how to implement them effectively in your investment journey.

Reference

- Bank for International Settlements (2023). Derivatives and Forex Markets Overview Report.
- Bloomberg (2024). Technology Sector Volatility Report.
- Charles Schwab (2023). Investor Insights and Funding Recommendations Report.
- CFA Institute (2023). Investor Behavior and Emotional Trading Study.
- Financial Conduct Authority (2023). Retail Forex Trading Risk Report.
- Financial Industry Regulatory Authority (FINRA) (2023). Brokerage Fees and Trading Behavior Analysis.
- Financial Industry Regulatory Authority (FINRA) (2024). Market Liquidity and Secondary Markets Study.
- Investment Company Institute (ICI) (2023). Mutual Fund and IRA Ownership Report.
- J.D. Power (2024). Investor Preferences in Brokerage Selection Survey.
- Morningstar (2023). Expense Ratios for ETFs and Mutual Funds Report.
- National Association of Real Estate Investment Trusts (NAREIT) (2023). REIT Market Overview and
- Dividend Yield Report.
- Options Clearing Corporation (OCC) (2023). Options Trading Volume Report.
- PitchBook (2023). Private Equity Investment Trends Report.
- Renaissance Capital (2023). IPO Market Trends Report.
- Securities and Exchange Commission (SEC) (2023). Primary Market Fundraising and Investor Protection
- Report.

- S&P Dow Jones Indices (2023). S&P 500 Historical Performance Study.
- World Economic Forum (2023). Blockchain Technology Impact Report.
- World Federation of Exchanges (2025). Global Stock Exchange Statistics Report.
- International Organization of Securities Commissions (IOSCO) (2023). Price Discovery Mechanisms in
- Secondary Markets.
- SEBI (2024). Equity Derivatives Trading Behavior Study in India.

The journey into stock market investing can be daunting for newcomers, yet with the right foundation, anyone can cultivate financial growth and make sound investment choices. This guide serves as a comprehensive introduction tailored for individuals without prior experience, simplifying intricate financial ideas into digestible lessons. It begins by outlining the fundamental principles of the stock market, detailing how businesses secure funding through Initial Public Offerings (IPOs) and how shares are exchanged on prominent platforms such as NYSE, NASDAQ, and NSE. Various market types—including primary, secondary, derivatives (futures and options), forex, commodities, and cryptocurrencies—are also examined.

Readers will gain insights into various investment vehicles like stocks, bonds, ETFs, mutual funds, and REITs while learning practical skills such as opening brokerage accounts and executing different order types (market, limit, stop-loss). The book delves into fundamental analysis techniques for assessing companies through financial statements and key performance ratios. Additionally, it introduces technical analysis tools that help in recognizing market trends through indicators like candlestick patterns and moving averages.

Advanced concepts include trading strategies involving futures and options while exploring investor psychology to understand how emotions can sway market behavior. Risk management is emphasized throughout the text to guide new investors in balancing potential rewards against risks while avoiding common pitfalls such as emotional decision-making or overtrading.

Ultimately, this book equips readers with a clear framework to navigate both long-term wealth-building strategies—like value investing—and short-term trading tactics. By blending theoretical knowledge with practical insights from seasoned investors' experiences, it fosters a disciplined approach to investing that values patience and strategic thinking.